SNOW WHITE'S PEOPLE: VOLUME ONE

An Oral History of the Disney Film
Snow White and the Seven Dwarfs

DAVID JOHNSON

Theme Park Press
www.ThemeParkPress.com

Editor: Bob McLain
Layout: Artisanal Text
Cover Photo: Courtesy of Bob Cowan

The cover photo, from the Ingeborg Willy collection, depicts Marge Champion, Disney's live-action reference for Snow White.

ISBN 978-1-68390-054-2
Printed in the United States of America

Theme Park Press | www.ThemeParkPress.com
Address queries to bob@themeparkpress.com

Contents

Foreword

David Johnson wrote a book about the making of *Snow White and the Seven Dwarfs* and a book about the Great Depression. It is a huge book. It is an ill-fated book, and a book that has yet to be released. It is a book for which David conducted dozens of interviews with "Snow White's people," the men and women who worked on Disney's cinematic masterpiece, many of whom had never been interviewed before or since.

A decade ago, when I read David's interview with director Wilfred Jackson, on animationartist.com, I was hooked. I decided that I wanted to find a way to read all of David's interviews. I was lucky enough to achieve that goal, a few years later, thanks to David's generosity. But this was still not enough. I knew that other Disney historians and Disney history enthusiasts needed to have access to those interviews and I lobbied David, month after month, year after year, to release his research in book form.

Then, a year ago, I learned from Bob McLain, the owner of Theme Park Press, that David had embraced the idea and had asked if I would be willing to write the foreword of his book. Would I be willing? I would have begged for that honor.

Sadly, over the years, not all of David Johnson's original interviews survived. Some of the recordings were preserved in their entirety, some only as excerpts. All of them contain information that is of utmost value to understand the making of *Snow White and the Seven Dwarfs*.

When my good friend and fellow Disney historian Todd James Pierce finished digitizing all the tapes that David could locate, we realized that, thankfully, so much material had actually been preserved that we were faced with an embarrassment of riches. This is why we decided to split the interviews into two volumes, the first of which you hold in your hands, and the second one of which will be released later this year.

One note of caution before turning the page: while reading these testimonies it is important to always keep in mind that no statement from any interview should ever be considered as the absolute truth, since the interviewee might have misremembered the facts, may have seen only part of the project described, or may have his own personal reasons for representing reality in a certain way. Hence the importance of the various perspectives provided in these books.

With this in mind, you are now ready to start your journey, to look behind the curtain and to meet the first of "Snow White's people."

Didier Ghez
Coral Gables, July 2016

Introduction

It has been so many years since I conducted the interviews presented here that, with my current life in Greece, I had almost forgotten them. Almost. For in the back of my mind I had hoped the bulk of them would be made available to a wider audience (in book form), to be read be many who would then relive those wonderful, long-lost days at Hyperion, where the greatest animated films, e.g., *Bambi* and *Fantasia*, were made and gestated. Thanks to Bob McLain and his generosity and patience, some of my "Snow White" dream has been fulfilled.

Re-reading these pages brings back many memories: Elly Horvath, then in her nineties, in her small house in Hemet, California, getting up from her chair and going to her small electric piano and playing and singing for me; Will Jackson, whose wife had so recently passed away and yet was able to summon up the strength of spirit to cope (even enthusiastically) with the barrage of questions I put to him; Eloise Tobelmann, at 82, yet so full of vigor and vitality for life; Grace Godino, a perennially youthful woman in her late 70s, who began to break down in tears of joy upon describing the initial studio-wide screening of a still-very unfinished *Snow White*; Art Babbitt, always embittered and prickly, whose generous wife insisted that I stay for dinner (she always called him "Bones"); Grim Natwick, who at 98 years of age still had a pair of the most beautiful bright blue eyes that I had ever seen and a mind still alert and overflowing with fascinating details of the past; Libbie Meador, one of the most generous and warm people who ever lived, and who practically adopted me from the start; Erna Englander, in and out of cancer remission, yet never allowing this to prevent our meetings which soon blossomed into a unique friendship; Shamus Culhane, who (like me) was trying to learn ancient Greek if only (also like me) because he felt that that language contained some of the greatest works ever conceived.

Early on in my research into the making of *Snow White* I realized that its creation depended upon two things: the Great Depression and

Walt Disney himself. The former brought to his doorstep countless individuals (many of whom were themselves geniuses) who would never have thought of a cartoon studio as a workplace in more opportune times yet remained and contributed a priceless input to something then considered an inferior form of artistic expression with little business potential. Walt was always something of an enigma. In the words of his long-time confidant and personal nurse Hazel George:

> A complex and interesting man, totally unspoiled by his fame—on certain levels he was almost a hick and on others ultra sophisticated. ... He had an individual belief that the origin of creativeness and effort was discontent. That was something that was unique to his way of thinking.

Certainly not something Max Flesicher would have pondered. And while he obviously needed and used the talent around him, Walt made his men, not the other way around. He guided and inspired them to infuse their drawings with life. He labored with them in fashioning a distinct personality for each newly created character. This applied not only to looks or speech but for every movement, down to the last flick of a finger. He was a true revolutionary, and in the words of Erna Englander, "a visionary."

Through these pages it is my hope that the reader will learn about not only *Snow White* but its creator as well. Though not perfect, Walt was far from the labels (anti-Semitic, ultra-right conservative, uneducated farm-boy) that still cling to a persona and individual the world could well benefit from today. Walt and the world of the imagination he created will in all likelihood never be seen again.

Wilfred Jackson (1906-1988)

As Frank Thomas and Ollie Johnston wrote in *Disney Animation: The Illusion of Life*, "Jaxon was easily the most creative of the directors, but he was also the most "picky" and took a lot of kidding about his thoroughness."

Frank Thomas recalled:

> Only a few people knew that "Jaxon" had any other name, and fewer still knew that it was "Wilfred." As a kid growing up in Glendale, that first name caused him considerable trouble and he claims that he survived only because he could run faster than anyone else. A classmate, Marion Morrison, also had a name with inherent problems, but he was bigger and no one picked on him. Even so, he chose the nickname "Duke" and later on even changed the whole name to John Wayne. Wilfred settled for "Jaxon."

Wilfred Jackson was also one of the best interviewees due to the thoroughness of his answers, and one can regret that he was not able to give as many interviews as Ward Kimball.

Born in Chicago, January 24, 1906, Wilfred E. Jackson attended Otis Art Institute in Los Angeles beginning in 1925. Three years later, just before Charlie Mintz had stolen Disney's Oswald the Lucky Rabbit character, he began hanging around The Walt Disney Studios. It was a poor time to ask for a job, but he volunteered to wash cels and assist animators until one day he found himself holding a paycheck. He later said, "I'm the only guy [at Disney] who was never hired."

He quickly moved up the ranks to animator, contributing to the Silly Symphony shorts. After *Steamboat Willie*, Jaxon went on to direct 35 shorts, three of which won Academy Awards: *The Tortoise and The Hare*, *The Country Cousin*, and *The Old Mill*. Probably the greatest example of his skill in developing action to music, however, was *The Band Concert* starring Mickey Mouse.

Jaxon also applied his talent to 11 animated features, including *Snow White and the Seven Dwarfs, Pinocchio, Dumbo, Saludos Amigos, Melody Time, Cinderella, Alice in Wonderland, Peter Pan,* and *Lady and the Tramp*. He directed such memorable sequences as "The Night on Bald Mountain" in *Fantasia,* and all cartoon and combination live-action footage in *Song of the South*. During the war years, he also produced and directed government films for the U.S. Navy.

Jaxon's consuming personal involvement in his films and his innate intensity finally caught up with him in 1953, when he suffered a heart attack which kept him away from the studio for most of a year. In 1954, as Walt entered the new television medium, he asked Jaxon to produce and direct animated shows on the *Disneyland* series. During the next four years, Jaxon directed 13 shows, including *The Story of the Animated Drawing*. But the pressure of working on the live-action stage for these shows became too stressful, and in the fall of 1959 he began a leave of absence which ended in his retirement two years later.

Wilfred Jackson died August 7, 1988, in Newport Beach, California.

David Johnson: Was the soundtrack [of "The Silly Song"] when it was being filmed just a piano accompaniment?

Wilfred Jackson: To the best of my recollection it was originally to a piano track. Now whether they made a preliminary orchestral take of that I'm not sure. I don't recall it being orchestra. That early in the cartoons we didn't usually pre-score music.

DJ: Would Frank [Churchill] have been there playing live or would they have done a loop for the soundtrack when they filmed this, for study purposes?

WJ: Probably a piano track.

DJ: By him playing it for you [live] or it being already recorded?

WJ: More likely [the latter], but it was done either way.

DJ: Now, besides the entertainment section, what others parts of the movie did you direct?

WJ: The other one that comes to mind is the scene toward the end of the picture where the dwarfs are gathered around the [casket].

DJ: From there to the end of the movie?

WJ: Yes. I'm vague on whether I had any other sequences in animation. You see, in those days we worked closely in connection with the story department during the development of the various sequences, and I was in the story work and in on the preparation for animation for so many different parts of the picture, but those two are the only ones that I recall actually directing.

DJ: So what exactly does a director do? I know you were in charge of some of the live action. But what else does a director do?

WJ: You're speaking strictly of *Snow White*?

DJ: Right.

WJ: First of all, as the story work was nearing completion.... You're familiar with storyboards? As they were being prepared and hauled over and beginning to take shape, after a series of meetings with Walt and the story group, the director would work in there and get his ideas incorporated into the thing, then the sequence would be delivered to the director to begin his work. His first task was to time each scene and visualize the choreography of the action—what action went with what parts of the music, if it was a musical sequence, or, as in the ending here, [prior to the closing with the song "Some Day My Prince Will Come"] there would be a pre-recording of the dialogue of all the vocal sounds. The director would be in on that usually. Having recorded those sounds, the director would see to it that the whole thing was timed, put together on a sound track. If there was music involved the director would play out the scenes ... where you have this scene and you cut to a close-up, and then you cut to something else and so forth, working with the layout man to prepare the visualization of the thing. Timing it was a matter of seeing if there was the right amount of time for all the different actions that had to take place and the pacing of the scene. The director, in effect, served as the film editor, pre-cutting the picture before it was made. Does that make sense?

DJ: Yes, it makes sense

WJ: There's a reason for that: because of the terrific expense. The pace of this particular sequence [where the prince comes down to pay his last respects] ... I believe that the sound was pre-recorded on that song and so it was my task, partly, to time the picture in such a way that it would look all right with the pre-determined length of the thing. Sometimes we would have to cut out actions that had been visualized and agreed on. Once in a while we would have to find some way of inserting action or expanding scenes in order for it to come out [correctly]. The music at the ending I'm not sure whether that was pre-recorded or not, when she rides away on the horse.

DJ: Do you recall some of the discussions on this particular scene and how it would work? For instance the animals would bow their heads, and the dwarfs do likewise, and Grumpy goes up and put the flowers on Snow White. Whose idea was it for Grumpy to go up and put flowers on Snow White?

WJ: Goodness, that idea originated in the story department early, before I picked the scene up, so I can't say. Let me say this about *Snow White*. The directors of *Snow White* didn't direct in the same way as they did on other pictures. In effect, Walt really directed that picture. He was so intensely involved in everything about it. And he was right in on everything that was done, right down to what color a character was painted. On *Snow White*, Walt was in on every last detail. It was Walt's picture, one hundred percent from beginning to end. That can't be said of any other picture that I've worked with him on after the very, very early Mickeys and Silly Symphonies, very early.

DJ: So that could have been Walt's idea?

WJ: It could have been. It could have been somebody in the story department. My goodness, Walt talked to everybody about his pictures. He shaped them up that way. He talked to the gardener or the janitor or anybody he could get hold of. He worked the thing out in his own mind by telling and re-telling and re-telling the thing, bouncing it off of anybody. If you had an idea, he would listen to it.

DJ: Were you involved in the very early stages of *Snow White*, say in late 1934, and taken off of the shorts and put in as...?

WJ: No, quite to the contrary. I was very busy keeping animators busy and I was working on shorts during the preparation of *Snow White* and not able to spend as much time as I would like to have with the story then. I was terribly interested in our first feature, of course. I was kept quite busy with short subjects during all the early preparation of it and to a much greater extent than in later feature work the story was quite well prepared, quite well rounded out in pretty much detail before I was involved in any of the sequences.

Snow White was a unique picture in the way it was made. No other picture was made like that at the studio during my time.

DJ: Do you recall if there was a pilot scene prepared?

WJ: Yes. The pilot sequence, the very first pilot sequence I saw, was the one where the dwarfs ... one scene or two or three scenes, where Snow White was asleep in the dwarfs' bed and they came in and they were all around the bed there and they were ready to attack the monster, and she makes a little sound and moved and they all shot down behind the front of the bed and then they came up one after another with their noses popping up. That was the pilot scene.

DJ: Did you, as a director, write out the dialogue on the exposure sheets that were then given to the animators, I mean on your own sequences?

WJ: Yes.

DJ: So that those sheets are in your handwriting?

WJ: It could be or in my assistant's handwriting.

DJ: And Bill Cottrell would have written the dialogue on the sheets he afterward gave Art Babbitt?

WJ: Yes. He wouldn't put the dialogue reading on.

DJ: What's the dialogue reading?

WJ: The dialogue reading is the visual interpretation of the frames of dialogue. On the exposure sheet each line represents one frame. One of the cutters in the cutting department would put headphones on and run the dialogue on the moviola, scoring it down with a little pencil and make marks [for exactly how long each syllable would take]. He would lay that out on the master exposure sheet and if there was a lot of dialogue in a sequence it was my practice to take the dialogue readings that I got from the cutter after we had the whole thing put in order and timed the way we thought it was going to be. I would lay my action out first of all on that before putting it on the exposure sheet. Then the task of transposing the dialogue reading we got from the film editor onto the animator's exposure sheet was handled by the assistant director. I have my scene cuts all indicated on the cutter's dialogue reading and the assistant director would lay out each scene on the exposure sheet. He wouldn't begin the thing at the top of the sheet: he would leave a little room for me to adjust the beginning of the scene, and at the end of the scene I could always add or subtract something I wanted to. He would lay it out with the scene number and the music room with all the different headings at the top. Those would probably be in my assistant's handwriting—not necessarily but probably. And that would be what I would use to indicate the action over in the action column—the vertical column at the extreme left. I would describe what goes on so that the animator would know where those different things came. Now this last step of actually laying the action on the exposure sheet was usually not done by the director by himself. First of all, if music was in any way involved closely with the action—which it was on almost all our early pictures including *Snow White* and *Pinocchio*—there was a musician in the director's room to work with him.

DJ: That's why it was called the music room?

WJ: Yes. That's why we call it that. And the musician would play music that was to be with the action over and over for the director to listen to and work with and to make adjustments with. So we would each know what the thing was to be like. We'd each make our suggestions until the musician was satisfied that he had something that made sense musically and the director was satisfied that the action could fit within the timing. This was very preliminary, of course. How much of that was done on *Snow White* I couldn't tell you. The sequences I had were pretty well worked out ahead of time, as far as music is concerned. Churchill [*Snow White*'s key song writer] and Larry Morey, who wrote the lyrics, would work together and present to the story department in a meeting with Walt their proposal of what music and words and sounds would go with the action, the business that the story department had on the storyboard. That was pretty well worked out ahead of time on the sequences I had. And all the yodeling, for instance, and that sort of thing, already had been recorded by Churchill or some other musician and worked out with the story department so that a great deal of what a director does on some of the other pictures wasn't done on my sequences on *Snow White*. That's why I say that it was sort of a different approach from the average, because of Walt's close involvement.

DJ: Now was it Fred Moore who did the dwarfs on your sequence?

WJ: Well, some of the scenes. There were others who also helped. Bill Tytla did the opening scene of the sequence and who was the one who did so many Dopey scenes?

DJ: Frank Thomas?

WJ: No.

DJ: Not Fred Moore?

WJ: No, he was kind of the creator of the dwarfs. [Jackson is almost certainly referring to animator Fred Spencer.] In any event, you're correct in thinking that Fred took the lead on the dwarfs. It was our practice to give the more important scenes to the more capable animators and to augment their work with scenes that were not as important to the picture—action scenes, longer shots, group shots, things like that, where the individual personality wasn't the most important part of the scene.

DJ: Did you do that yourself? Did you allocate which scenes went to which animator?

WJ: To a certain extent. Walt had a big hand in that on the *Snow White* picture. I probably had less to say about who did what in *Snow White* than in any other picture I directed. Walt, as I said, was in on every detail.

DJ: Can you think of anything from the movie that was your idea and that made it into the picture?

WJ: Aside from the details, the choreography of what the action was to encompass was my major contribution, I would think. Plus the timing of it: how long a scene would be, where it would come in juxtaposition with other scenes.

DJ: For instance, the dancing style of the dwarfs, almost like a square dance, that was your idea?

WJ: I don't think I approached it that way. We pictured the dwarfs as sort of folksy characters and very probably I was thinking more of a mixture of country-style Americana with a European flavor. As to the individual actions in that case, I don't have a specific recollection of any of those things.

DJ: And I suppose the sneeze was already pre-determined, probably by Walt.

WJ: The sneeze was definitely worked out before I took the sequence up, even to the extent of having recorded a whole bunch of different sneezes. Selecting which sneeze, which part of which sneeze went where, was very much in my hands. But I was working with a track that was already [made]. I was more like a film editor in relation to that. What they did, all those different things [such as the close-ups of the hands clapping as the scene reached its climax with the sneeze] were suggested by the story sketches and by the continuity on the storyboard, and there were variations of what was done and what was done when. That is, the sequence of action was mine. What I put together was not exactly what was on the storyboard, a, b, c, d, e, f, g. And the pacing of it was mine, the building of the excitement, the increase in tempo, making the scenes shorter than the previous ones: that sort of thing, that was mine.

DJ: Was this sequence difficult and did you have any problems in getting it going the way you wanted it?

WJ: I suppose I had. No individual particular problems stand out in my mind other than getting enough work ready for animators fast enough to keep them busy. Trying to meet our deadlines, but that was for all our pictures. I don't recall problems with this sequence. It was just a joy to work on.

DJ: Did they film other actors for the dwarfs, besides yourself I mean?

WJ: Yes, different ones. The fellas would do things. Perce Pearce did a pretty good Doc and was filmed for some of it. We used to have meetings, a whole bunch of us animators and directors would come back at night and we'd have a meeting over on the soundstage. We'd talk about the characters. We'd talk about what they were like and how they would act and how they would move and anybody who wanted to would get up and demonstrate his idea of what the guy should move like, how he should do this particular thing.

DJ: It's interesting that you came in at night, after work. Was this a lot?

WJ: Oh, yes. We had all kinds of meetings at night. This wasn't just on *Snow White*, but especially along about then. We had classes that we attended. Walt hired people from outside to come and teach us, [like] Don Graham to teach the animators.

DJ: Did you go to those classes?

WJ: No, because I wasn't one of the artists at that time.

DJ: When you first came to the studio, were you hired as an artist?

WJ: Yes, I was sort of hired as a pest that Walt hired to get out of his office. I was very persistent.

DJ: Now you came in 1928 or 1929?

WJ: [April 1928], you're right; 1929 was when we were married. I had met Jane who became my wife in art school when I was at the County Art Institute, now Otis Parsons, and we'd been going together and we liked each other a lot and we were quite serious about getting married. I needed a job and I had always wanted to be a cartoonist. I had wanted to be in animation. But as far as I knew the only animating studios were in New York City and I didn't have a way of getting to New York City. I hadn't finished my art school education. I wasn't really a very good draughtsman. I needed a lot more study before I would become [one], but I found out by accident that there was a person in Hollywood who made cartoons named Walt Disney. One of the girls at the Art Institute had a boyfriend who was working for Walt Disney and from her I got the name and the phone number of the place. I called Walt up and asked for an interview. I didn't know until afterwards that I hit Walt for a job right at the time when he had discovered that he had lost the rights to this Oswald character. He didn't have anything else going yet. He was in a transition from that to the Mickeys. He granted me an interview. I came in with my samples and showed them to him and he said, "You really aren't ready to take a job as an animator yet. You don't draw well enough. You need more training in drawing." I said "All right, now I'm going to be an animator someday. What should I study at art school? Where should I go and what should I study in order to learn how to be an animator?" He said "There isn't really any place you can learn to be an animator, except at an animation studio. They don't teach it anywhere that I know of." I said "All right, that's fine. How would it be if I come to your studio and learn to be an animator here and I'll pay you tuition, like I would have to pay at any other school?" And he said "Well, godammit Jack, I can't do a thing like that!" Finally he said, "Look, come in on Monday and we'll see if you can do anything useful around here." I came in on

Monday and they kept me busy helping the janitor cleaning off the ink lines and paint off of the cels and separating the ones that were too scratched from the ones that weren't too scratched. It was shortly after that that everybody left the studio except Iwerks, Les Clark, and Johnny Cannon, and for a while there was a Mike [Marcus] who ran the camera. In any event, I counted that I was the thirteenth one when I was hired, so I figured that thirteen must be my lucky number. Naturally, when Walt began to hire people from the East, like Ben Sharpsteen, Jack Campbell, Norm Ferguson, Tom Palmer, and those guys, they were such great animators and so much better draughtsman that I wasn't really filling the bill very well. I had worked up to the point that I was doing animation.

DJ: Not just inbetweening, you were actually animating?

WJ: Yes, I was doing my own scenes, and I wasn't doing too well. I didn't know that. I didn't realize how poor my work was compared to the others, and I used to come back at night. Walt encouraged us to come back if we wanted to and to animate our own scenes, our own ideas, and to show them to him. I was back one night doing that and Walt got into a little trouble editing and putting sound to one of the pictures. I helped Walt work out their method of synchronizing.

DJ: The metronome, right?

WJ: Yes. I helped him tie the sound up with the picture and I helped him with some things like that. And I'd had a little bit of time working on the editing of the pictures and that sort of thing. One night when I went back there.... I wanted to animate a whole picture myself—I was that conceited. I thought I could do it. I was interested in animation. I liked to make the characters move on the screen. That was what I wanted to do. And I said: "Walt, sometime if it would work out, I'd like to handle a whole picture, if you see a way to let me try it." I used the wrong word. I meant "animate." He thought I meant direct or produce. I didn't find out till after he had already decided to try me out on it that we had a misunderstanding about it. I was in there happily animating some scenes and he sends Rudy Zamora in and Rudy said, "Walt told me to come in and get some scenes from you. I'm out of work." I thought, "Gee wiz, here it goes, I'm not going to get to animate the whole picture after all and Walt said I could do it."

DJ: What short was it?

WJ: This was *The Castaway*. It was a picture when Walt was behind on schedule and needed something to catch up with, and he had a lot of footage that had been cut out of other cartoons and it was saved in the morgue. All the animation was done, and my first job was to make some kind of a story where we could use all this discarded stuff. The only way I could see to tie all this stuff together was to have Mickey be cast away on an island after his ship was wrecked and to be sort of a Robinson Crusoe character and had all kinds of materials that had come from the ship, including a piano, and all the things that were needed for all the different scenes. It would be on an island where there were jungle creatures to use gags about and jungle animals in the various out footage. Walt had hired a musician when he put me to work on the thing. He said: "I got a new musician I just hired and I want you to work with him on your picture. I want to see if he's any good and if we can use him." I said, "Fine." That musician happened to be Frank Churchill.

DJ: Could you tell me a little about Frank Churchill. Did he ever tell you, for instance, what his musical influences were? Did he like Mozart or Beethoven, or was it Tchaikovsky or Wagner?

WJ: The only thing that comes to mind there right off…. I recall one time Frank saying something about Schubert's use of melody. Melody was the thing about Schubert that was so arresting. I don't recall Frank telling me much about his influences.

DJ: Would you say that he liked classical music or did he prefer popular music as a musician himself?

WJ: Frank had great facility in playing either on the piano. Frank was a pianist. He was a pianist more than he was a composer.

DJ: Really?

WJ: Yes. Before he came to Walt to work, he had been playing mood music and when sound came in they didn't need this. He had been playing sad music when the actors were supposed to be acting sad, and happy music when they were supposed to be happy, to help them with their acting. He had a little folding organ that folded all up. It had a bellows that you pumped with your feet like this, and he didn't have any use for it anymore so he gave it to me. I had that for many years. The girls used to play with it. Working with Frank was so different from working with Leigh Harline, for instance.

DJ: I know that Leigh Harline was the more sophisticated musician.

WJ: Yes, he was a composer first, and he played the piano sort of like doing the pick-and-shovel work. Frank, when he sat down at the piano and played the music that you were working out for the picture, the score that resulted never sounded any better than the way Frank played it on the piano. With Leigh Harline you had to learn to make allowances for the fact that you'd hear the melody he was playing when the thing was done, but the feeling of it, the mood that it would create, the feeling that it would extend to you, wasn't there with the piano. You just had to trust Leigh that it was going to sound a whole lot different after he orchestrated it.

DJ: Did these composers do their own orchestration or did they have another person [do it]? For instance, did Churchill actually orchestrate his songs or did he have an assistant [do it]?

WJ: He very possibly did, in the very early days, but it wouldn't have been long before they would have had someone to orchestrate.

DJ: And you wouldn't recall who that might have been for *Snow White*?

WJ: No. We already had expanded the music department quite a bit by that time. I'm not sure if Al Malotte was there already or Paul Smith.

DJ: Paul Smith worked on some of the incidental music on *Snow White*. Did Leigh Harline do his own orchestrations, since he was a composer?

WJ: He would have been much more likely to have done it.

DJ: It's amazing that Churchill wrote so many memorable songs and yet as you say, he wasn't really a composer. He must have had a lot of talent under his belt.

WJ: Frank was something else when it came to working with him.

DJ: What was he like?

WJ: Frank was just a fun person to work with. He did what he did with such apparent ease, and he was so willing to adapt his music, to change it to what you needed. He seemed to be able to take notes out or add notes in and still make it work. If you're having a little trouble fitting your action to the music, he had great facility in adjusting the music and still make it come out right. He had such a variety of different tunes, of different things that he could suggest when you were first working with him on a short subject. You'd have a sequence of action and you'd talk to him about it and the feeling of it and so forth and he'd suggest music for it and if you didn't like it he'd suggest something else and he could just go on and on and on and on.

DJ: Could he remember the music without writing it down, like if you preferred one of the earlier options?

WJ: I don't recall he had any trouble if you wanted one of the earlier suggestions he played. He'd play something: "Was this it? Was that it?" "Yeah, that was it," and we'd work on that one. However, when we selected a tune, he'd write down a melody line with a signature on it. We'd have that to come back to.

DJ: Do you remember any of his pranks? I understand he was very playful. Shamus Culhane told me he liked to sit at the piano and fart and then pick out the note and put that in the song.

WJ: Yes. [Laughs]

DJ: That's true, then?

WJ: Yes. Also, he and Earl Duval got caught by one of the secretaries when she came in the room, trying to light one. He was bent over and Earl was there with a match. The minute the door opened, Frank said, "Where is that knife? I dropped that knife here somewhere?"[Laughs]

DJ: Who was the secretary?

WJ: Carolyn Shafer. She later on married Frank.

DJ: Oh, that was Walt's secretary.

WJ: Yes. I have a knife that Frank Churchill gave me, which was the knife he said he was looking for. He picked it out of a claw machine.

DJ: Claw machine? Oh, yes, I remember those, in the amusement parks.

WJ: Yes, you put your nickel in and it grabs some candy, but there're also little things in there. Frank was very good at operating that thing. He used to like to show off and say, "What do you want out of there?" Whoever was with him would say, "See if you can get that." And he was very good at getting the thing over and grabbing it and it pleased him that he could do that better than practically everyone else.

Another thing I remember about Frank and the playful end of it was seeing him on a driving range hitting golf balls. He had the most unprofessional stance I have ever seen. He played with both knees bent sort of in a half squat, and he didn't have the twist that other people had. He hit the ball like you would with a hockey stick or a baseball bat, and he'd give the thing a vicious cut. He could send it a long way from where he wanted it. He was good at it, but I don't mean professionally. He couldn't get out with the real pros, but compared with the friends he played with he was good. I didn't play myself, but often would go with him and Earl Duvall.

DJ: Who was Earl Duvall?

WJ: He was one of our early storymen, an artist and an idea man. He had made layouts with me for a while and that's how come he and Frank were together in the music room the time Frank was looking for his knife. There were a lot of pranks going on. Walt didn't discourage it. We didn't just clown around, we worked hard. But Walt didn't measure your value to the studio by whether you had your nose down to the grindstone for exactly eight hours every day. It was the contribution you made: as long as you got your job done and didn't interfere with anybody else getting their job done, how long you took and when you did it didn't matter.

I got in there, as I told you, very accidentally. I got into directing pictures without meaning to. I had absolutely no qualifications for being a director, none whatsoever. I had few enough to be an animator. But Walt didn't understand that anybody who wanted to couldn't do anything they wanted to do. He didn't understand that other people couldn't. So I spent the rest of my years there doing a job I didn't know how to do, working up a plow horse to try to keep up with the race horse and putting in a lot of extra hours in order to come out even.

DJ: You're very modest. Some of your work is considered the greatest work ever done.

WJ: That may be others' opinions, it's not mine.

DJ: You did *The Old Mill*, I understand.

WJ: Yes.

DJ: That's just one of your highlights.

WJ: I loved to work with musicians. I like musical pictures.

DJ: Getting back to what you said about your nose to the grindstone. Did Walt have deadlines, let's say, for *Snow White*? When he put you there to direct some of these scenes and to get them to the animators, was there a deadline, like, by April first this scene had to be given out to the animators. Was there anything like that going on?

WJ: Not that kind of a deadline. Not scene by scene. When scenes went to animators [the deadline] was dictated by when the animator who was to do that scene finished what he was doing before. The cardinal sin was to let an animator be out of work. There were deadlines for the pictures and deadlines for the individual sequences within the picture as to when they should go to camera as far as the director was concerned. These deadlines could be, and often were, adjusted by the time we didn't meet out deadlines.

DJ: That must have been especially true on a picture like *Snow White*?

WJ: Yes. Could I digress and tell you a little thing about *Snow White*?

DJ: Please.

WJ: When Walt started to make *Snow White*, everybody that he talked to in Hollywood, all the best advice he could get, was discouraging. The consensus was that nobody would sit still to watch a cartoon, a feature-length cartoon: the audiences would walk out on it. With that in mind Walt went ahead and made *Snow White* and we had the preview, I believe at the Carthay Circle Theater.

DJ: That's correct. December 21, 1937.

WJ: You know more about *Snow White* than I do. In any event, the picture was partway through when some people got up and started to walk out.

DJ: Oh, you're talking about the preview. I think the preview was at a Fox theater.

WJ: You've heard of this then.

DJ: They had to get back for a final exam or something.

WJ: Yeah they had to get back to school, but Walt thought....

DJ: He must have been devastated. You all must have been devastated.

WJ: Yeah. It was a bad moment.

DJ: When did you finally find out?

WJ: Walt decided he'd better go out into the foyer and listen and see what they were saying when they went out. He got out there and ran into the theater manager who explained to him what was going on so he didn't have to commit suicide. [Laughs]

DJ: Do you remember the big story meeting when Walt got together several artists one night and acted out the whole story of *Snow White*, even acting the animal parts?

WJ: That would be par for the course on any picture. When we would have our story meetings, Walt would get up and act things out to demonstrate what he had in mind, like the little baby bear that needed to break something and would pick up a rock and tip too far back with it. And Walt acted it out and fell backwards on his chair.

DJ: I notice that in the early story stages of *Snow White* that there are a lot of comical routines that were later dropped, like the early arrival of the prince, who originally serenades Snow White with his mandolin while his horse watches the proceedings from the wall, one front leg bent at the knee under his chin. I suppose that since the shorts were mainly comical, it would be natural that in the early stages, at least, *Snow White* would get a similar treatment.

WJ: We were all encouraged to make all kinds of suggestions. It didn't matter if we thought they were in line or not. Walt wanted any suggestions anybody had, of any sort.

DJ: Do you remember any particular thing that you thought of that was actually used in *Snow White*?

WJ: No, I don't. As I said, the sequences I had on *Snow White* were very well worked out before I got them. Very thoroughly worked out.

DJ: Do you recall who the script writers were for the scenes you did?

WJ: No, I don't recall. When you say script writers, we didn't have scripts, we had storyboards.

DJ: But wasn't it typed into scripts when the dialogue was to be recorded and also so it could be read and followed for each sequence?

WJ: That would be taken from the storyboard. Underneath the sketches was written the dialogue to be spoken during that scene.

DJ: Since you worked on *The Old Mill*, you were involved with the multiplane camera. Can you tell me about [Bill] Garity [the co-inventor] and the invention of this thing and some of the problems and miracles that it did.

WJ: What I can tell you about my experiences with it was that the *The Old Mill* was supposed to be a test of the mutiplane, to see if it worked. Somehow we were so held up in working on *The Old Mill* by assignments of animators, because *Snow White* was in work at that time and animators that I should have had were pulled away just before I got to them and other animators were substituted because *Snow White* got preference on everything. And we got our scenes planned and worked out for the multiplane effects and by that time some of the sequences on *Snow White* were being photographed. The multiplane camera itself had all kinds of bugs in it that had to be worked out. We were held up until so late that I actually did work on another short—I don't remember which short. I don't even remember if I finished it up. I did work on some other picture to keep myself busy while we could get facilities to go ahead on *The Old Mill*. By the time they had got the bugs out of the multiplane camera, they had multiplane scenes for *Snow White* to shoot and they got it busy on those first. Finally, in order to get *The Old Mill* out the scenes that had been planned for multiplane had to be converted to the flat camera to do the best they could. You won't find more than a very few multiplane scenes in *The Old Mill*.

DJ: I wasn't aware of that.

WJ: I've had messed-up schedules on pictures. but I've never had a more messed-up one than I can remember for *The Old Mill*.

DJ: Did you actually go to the camera yourself to see how it worked?

WJ: Oh, yes. All of us had our noses in everything that was going on at the studio all the time.

DJ: Can you tell me about some of the effects? They mentioned backlighting under the glass for some of the candle effects.

WJ: I don't know how that effect was worked out. I think there was a dark thing underneath with a pin hole in it and a light behind that.

DJ: Could you talk about the man who designed the multiplane camera, Bill Garity?

WJ: Yes. Bill Garity was a sound engineer. Was it the silent film *People in New York* where they worked out a system of recording sound? Bill Garity came with that system to the studio in the very, very early days. That was a system, a method of reproducing sound by horizontal dark lines in the sound track instead of a wiggly line; and the broader they were or narrower they were had to do with the loudness and softness. And the closeness together or fartherness apart had to do with the pitch. That was our first system that was used, and Bill Garity appeared with this marvelous thing at the studio and he stayed on until he was in charge of the sound for years and years.

DJ: Do you recall Walt ever discussing with you his plans for the multiplane or his discussing any dissatisfaction with the pictures or about getting more depth or realism?

WJ: Only in that it was one of the aspects of the pictures he always emphasized.

DJ: You mean the realism?

WJ: Yes. We faked that before we ever got to the multiplane by using sliding cels. We moved the foreground cel faster than the back cel.

DJ: Who figured that out?

WJ: My goodness, I don't know.

DJ: I thought maybe you did.

WJ: No. That was used quite awhile before I remember the concept of the multiplane camera. The multiplane camera was really just an extension of that, you know. It was a matter of instead of having the cels just on the flat bed and moving them differently, it was a matter of separating them. So that would automatically get the difference in speed, too. Instead of having to guess how it would look if you moved one 3/16 of an inch every frame, and the other one 1/8 of an inch every frame, instead of guessing at it you got a more realistic effect, because you were actually using perspective. But how and when and by whom that was conceived I really don't know. It's such a natural thing that probably more than one person had the idea. It was a matter of finding a way to make it work with the cartoons.

DJ: Garity seems to get credit for it. On the original U.S. patent drawings, Garity's name is given along with McFadden.

WJ: I don't recall that name.

DJ: Now here on this layout sketch is the term "Truck in cam[era] to 3 field." Would you as a director make that kind of decision, or for a truck in for a close up?

WJ: Essentially I would be responsible for it, but whether I would suggest it or whether the layout man would suggest it, I don't know. Our layout men were sort of the equivalent of a camera man in a live-action picture. They created the camera angles that were used.

DJ: I thought that was the director. I thought that was your job.

WJ: We worked together. But to actually put it down on paper it was their job to make *the* drawing that indicated the actual setup. A lot of it came right directly from the story department. You find two different sketches that obviously should be in the same scene by moving the camera. We all worked closely together. It's awfully hard to say whose idea anything was. It was a team effort.

DJ: So a typical day for you was to go to the studio. Where did you live at that time [when *Snow White* was in production]?

WJ: It's difficult to say. We moved quite a few times until 1936. Then we moved from a little apartment up on Hyperion [Avenue] right near the studio out to our three-acre place in what is now Sunland. We had owned it for quite some time and I didn't want to go in debt, so I was saving up enough money to build a little house on the place. We bought it years before. The builder, Frank Crowhurst, was the same one that built several of the buildings on Hyperion [Avenue] for Walt.

DJ: You drove to the studio?

WJ: Yes. Sunland is in the foothills north of North Hollywood—up in the Verdego Hills.

DJ: Did you have your own office at the time?

WJ: I was in the music room. I shared that with the musician, my assistant director.

DJ: Who was that?

WJ: Graham Heid I think was with me at that time.

DJ: And Churchill was there and Leigh Harline?

WJ: On *Snow White* I don't remember who the musician was in the music room. It wouldn't have been Churchill. Churchill and Larry Morey worked together in their own office in a different part of the building. There would have been some musician with me, quite possibly it was Leigh Harline. He was with me for many years.

DJ: He did a lot of the background music for *Snow White*.

WJ: Yes. He was with me on the shorts along about that time. Probably he was the musician. And in the adjoining room, with a door through so you wouldn't have to go out in the hallway, was the layout man's room. It would be the layout man with two or three assistants.

DJ: Why was the entertainment section that you were on so much fun, as you said?

WJ: Partly because we worked closer with Walt on that picture than any since the very early ones. Partly because it was a fun sequence. The gags were funny, the music was fun to work with. The problems we had were interesting ones to work out. The animators I worked with were great guys, everything.

DJ: Do you remember any of those interesting problems?

WJ: Just the adaptation of the business to the soundtrack. You got a storyboard there and you got a soundtrack and you got to make one fit the other. And there are a myriad of decisions that you have to make. Partly it was the excitement of the whole thing.

DJ: Would it be safe to say that you at least partly choreographed the dwarfs dancing around in your sequence?

WJ: Let me say this. It was my decision what would be done regardless of where the inspiration came from. It was my decision to decide which one of the possible actions would be used, within the limitations of what I understood from Walt. I tried to be an extension of Walt's fingers. I tried to put on film what I thought was in Walt's mind. The details, making it work, how it was to be done, were up to me. I didn't make Jackson pictures, I made Walt Disney pictures.

DJ: Yes, but it would have been different from someone else.

WJ: It would have been different. Maybe better.

DJ: I doubt it. And the last sequence was such a beautiful scene. It's interesting that you had that scene. Of all the movies that Disney

ever made, that sequence is the most uplifting. There's never an ending to any other picture that quite compares with the magic of the dwarfs jumping around and saying goodbye.

WJ: This wasn't fed by just that scene. This was done because Walt was able to create a picture that led up to that scene and in which the audience felt very strongly sympathetic to the dwarfs and to the little animals. It was through the empathy for the dwarfs that the picture was successful. Snow White as a character: what happened to her wouldn't have hit you with the same impact. You wouldn't have cared as much about what happened to her as how the dwarfs felt about it. So what is so good about that scene is the feeling that has been built up in the audience before they get to that scene plus some wonderful animation of the grieving dwarfs.

DJ: But the way you did it I still think was commendable.

WJ: It worked.

DJ: It certainly did work.

Interviewed in Winter 1988.

Bill Cottrell
(1906–1995)

Bill Cottrell was the first president of WED (known today as Walt Disney Imagineering). During the planning and construction phases of Disneyland, Walt relied heavily on Bill's creativity, wisdom, and foresight to make his dream come true.

Born to English parents in South Bend, Indiana, in 1906, Bill graduated with degrees in English and journalism from Occidental College in Los Angeles, California. After working on George Herriman's *Krazy Kat* comic strip for a time in 1929, he was offered a job working cameras at the Disney Studio.

He soon moved into the story department and contributed ideas to shorts, including *Who Killed Cock Robin?* Fellow Disney storyman Joe Grant recalled, "Bill was a great fan of Gilbert and Sullivan and you will see elements of that, such as the jury-box chorus, in *Who Killed Cock Robin?*"

Bill went on to direct the wicked witch and evil queen sequences in *Snow White and the Seven Dwarfs* and contributed to story on *Pinocchio*. In 1941, he joined Walt Disney and a small group of artists on the goodwill tour of South America, which inspired *The Three Caballeros* and *Saludos Amigos*, for which he also helped develop story. Bill also contributed to *Victory Through Air Power*, *Melody Time*, *Alice in Wonderland*, and *Peter Pan*.

During the 1950s, Bill carried his interest in story over to WED, where he helped develop story lines and dialog for such Disneyland attractions as *Snow White's Adventures*.

Bill was also keen on nomenclature. John Hench recalled, "He was a talented writer and helped shape how we referred to events and attractions at Disneyland. For instance, he encouraged us to quit using the term "ride" and to refer to attractions as an "experience," which is exactly what they are: an experience."

Among his many contributions to Disney, Bill also helped develop the popular *Zorro* television series, and in 1964 was named president of Retlaw Enterprises, the Walt Disney family corporation. He held that position until 1982 when he retired after 53 years of service. A life-long fan of Sherlock Holmes, Bill's idea of a movie about an animal detective inspired the 1986 animated feature *The Great Mouse Detective*.

Bill Cottrell died December 22, 1995, in Los Angeles.

David Johnson: Do you recall exactly what scenes you directed?

Bill Cottrell: Let me begin by saying [that the] story Joe Grant and I and Dorothy Ann Blank worked on was the queen, the mirror, the huntsman, the transformation of the witch, and the witch sequences. Now there may have been some special scenes in there that we didn't work on, I'm not sure, but basically those were the scenes that we developed in story. And then I went into direction and directed presumably those same scenes, but there may again have been some that were left out, because they may have overlapped with someone else's continuity of the dwarfs or something like that.

[Concerning Dorothy Ann Blank's work]

It was hard to develop the story in many respects. We were all so used to working on cartoons [and] we're getting into a cartoon story that's pretty much live action. I don't recall how much she had to rewrite. We all did. It was a matter of determining the personalities as we developed them. I think that had we have had the voices earlier it might have been easier to devise. Lucille Laverne came in.... We had interviewed or I had interviewed [more or less] twenty voices for the queen and the witch.

DJ: May I ask you who decided who to interview?

BC: A department, I presume, would do research and get people in, mostly from radio. It's like the casting director will seek out the people that he thinks might be the right voice. And no one really knows what the right voice is.

[Laverne] was mostly a stage actress. When the voices were brought in, there were radio shows that had witches in them, old crones. They all had a pattern that was a cliché, almost as if crones talk this way. "All of us crones talk alike. We all cackle and crack our voice," and so on. After seeing a bunch of these, they all seemed rather uninteresting because you'd heard the same thing on radio for so many years. Lucille Laverne was brought in late one afternoon, and she came in.

DJ: What was she like when she came in?

BC: She was almost brusque. This was a no-nonsense character. We had a storyboard on the soundstage. She came in and I told her what the character was and I had a script to test and I said, "Would you like to see the storyboard? Let me go through the story and show you what your character would be." She took the script from me and read it without looking at the storyboard. You could have made a take of that voice that she read as the queen.

DJ: And her voice in real life certainly wasn't like either one of them apparently, was it?

BC: She was a professional actress, and I think when she was told that the queen is a vain, imperialistic personality she visualized something. She read the lines beautifully and then when she went into the witch with the maniacal laugh, it rang all over the soundstage. It was blood curdling.

DJ: So you knew right at the first that....

BC: That was the one.

DJ: When you interviewed the others, did they do both parts? In other words, did you think of having one actress for both parts even then?

BC: I doubt it very much.

DJ: Because it would seem to me that she would have been thought of as perfect for the witch. Was it your or her idea that said, "Oh let me read the queen. I might be able to do that too."

BC: I don't remember. I couldn't tell you that for sure. Some of the others might have read the queen's lines, too. They were all radio actresses. They should have been able to do it. The queen's voice again: no one read it with any great authority or with anything outstanding. Lucille Laverne was *remarkable*. She came in at a time when [we had] gone through all the others and [were] wondering, "What are we going to do?" She came in and within a matter of a few minutes she was in, as far as I was concerned. Then we made a test of her voice and ran it for Walt. Same thing: he said, "That's it!" Lucille Laverne got the part and all throughout the takes that we made with her, we didn't have to make too many takes. She took direction well.

DJ: Was Walt present during the takes?

BC: I don't think so. He might have been, but I don't remember.

DJ: Because Ward [Kimball] thought that he might be since this was the first feature.

BC: He might have been. He wasn't there on the first test. He might have been on some of the other scenes.

DJ: What was Laverne like as a person? Did she have a lot of fun? Was she a cut-up? Did she like to joke around?

BC: I don't think so, not a great deal. She was rather serious and she lived in Pasadena, I believe. She wrote me a couple of times. I can only remember a couple of things. I think she asked a couple of questions about some property that she had that was being taxed more than she thought it was being fair and it was rather an argumentative letter about the tax system or something like that.

DJ: Why would she ask you about that?

BC: I don't know. I guess she wanted someone to talk to. I don't have the slightest idea. I can't say that I knew her well. I enjoyed her performance very much and I appreciated it and I enjoyed being with her on the set. But she wasn't like [Walter] Catlett [the voice of Fox in *Pinocchio*] who was just great when he got going. He'd just go on and on with great stories. He should have been recorded. Lucille was not that outgoing, at least not with me. I don't think with anyone. I think it was just a business thing: come in and shoot it and go home.

DJ: Would she have been in on any of the story meetings?

BC: No, everything was ready to be recorded when she came in. She wasn't in any meetings. I don't recall her any more than just a few sessions when the story was ready to go to direction.

We wanted to shoot live action of the character in costume to establish [them], particularly with the queen and the witch, to establish certain actions and motions rather than let the animator have to figure it all out. I don't know if they did it with any others or not, maybe they did. We were doing it to playback and she was not able to do it very well to playback. She just heard it and it's synced so that her action is synced with the voice so as she moves and as she ... particularly on the cauldron, for instance. Even though it was her own voice, somehow or other I think the timing confused her or something wasn't right. She was not used to that type of thing, so she would act the way she was thinking at the time, regardless of the voice. She was not in sync with the tempo. She was used to a stage play wherein she had time—depending on the director of the play—time to make a speech, time to make a move across the stage and so forth. We were working with a different type of timing that we understood. We have to do it in a certain number of frames. Your scene cannot ramble on forever. It has to be rather concise. So we had to get a substitute.

[A] very handsome, tall girl, like a model, did the queen and she was very good. Because again she doesn't have to do a lot off walking around. Her scenes were precise. She goes to the mirror, she asks the mirror a question. She reacts. There's not a lot of wandering around and ad-libbing and lighting a cigarette, like Bette Davis.

She did one scene that was great: we had a staircase for her, for the queen to go down into the dungeon. And she had a long, black velvet robe, and she looked great. She looked like the queen, like Joe Grant's drawing. She came down, and as she went around the stairway she took her cape and swirled it to follow her down there, and it opened up just beautifully. I can't describe it except that it was used in animation. You might say she invented that. Just by doing it she invented it. We didn't say, "Do this." She did it perhaps to keep her robe from dragging down the stairs or something. Maybe she thought it [looked] good. She did it in a rehearsal and [we'd] say, "Hey, that's great! Do that next time." We shot it. I always remember *that* scene as being an inventive thing from the actress.

Of course, once she got into the witch now you're into a cartoon character. I think we had more knowledge of how to make that character work than the queen. It was particularly difficult at that time for animators to animate a live-action character. The movement is rather slow, unless they're striding across the room. That means the drawings have to be accurate, then the tracings on celluloids have to be dead accurate or they're going to affect the animation slightly. The peg holes have got to be new and not wobbly and the cels the same way. There're so many things that can cause the paper or the celluloid to go awry between the times the animator does it, the inker does it.... The painter doesn't use the peg holes, so they're just painting the inked lines. Then even the camera department has got some cels that have to be taken care of very carefully.

Animation of the human figure was rather new. We hadn't had too much experience in it and not too much success in it. The queen was well done partly because she struck poses. She was not a hap-happy person. She was not laughing and moving around. She took a serious pose that you would imagine a queen in a fairy tale would. And so when she was talking to the mirror, for instance, she would just stand there and talk and then react.... In all that part of the picture the process was very enjoyable. I enjoyed it.

I'm inclined to think that a great deal of these scenes are determined by the story sketches as to how it's going to look. You have to plan a scene almost in advance. I think on the drawing board it showed [the queen] sitting, talking, standing up, and you come to a close-up to accentuate certain words or actions.

Before I was even directing those scenes [of the queen, etc.] I was in with the story all the time. Then when that was finished I went to directing. So you know by talking the scene endlessly what's going to happen. Then Walt comes in and he says, "Perhaps she ought to do this, she should stand up, she should do this." You've got different people saying, "Wouldn't it be great to do this and this," and you combine the best of them, and [in] your final story meeting with Walt or [in] any one of your meetings with Walt, pretty soon you're all talking about the same thing. You're all talking about how it's going to look. You don't have just a bunch of open scenes there with no accents to [them].

[Discussing his job as director on *Snow White*.]

I was on story first, which is continuity, writing the gags and so forth, whatever one would do to develop the continuity of the story. That's with the story department: it's like a writer who can draw.

DJ: That's what you did in the beginning.

BC: Yeah.

DJ: And how long would say that went on? Because *Snow White* went in fits and starts, didn't it? In the beginning they did a lot of gags and stories and stuff, and then they stopped because then they had to study animation and finally they got Marge Belcher and they did more animation and then they got more going.

BC: I couldn't tell you the number of months, but it was a full-time job.

DJ: Just on *Snow White*? Do you recall that once you got on *Snow White* you didn't spend much time on shorts?

BC: Joe Grant and I worked on short subjects together the first time we worked together. We had worked together but not as a team. We worked on pictures like *Three Orphaned Kittens*.

DJ: What was your day-to-day routine when doing your work on *Snow White*?

BC: It's kind of hard to say what the day to day was, but you know that you have a sequence to do and you know you've got the opening sequence with the queen, and so you develop that. I'm speaking now for all of us working on it. And the continuity of the whole picture is more or less outlined in where your sequences are. For instance, the introduction of the queen, when she finds out that Snow White is fairer than she and she sends for the huntsman. That's another sequence that we did. And the mirror prior to that the huntsman. And the huntsman, and then maybe we'd skip down the line quite a bit and pick up something else, still with the queen, when the huntsman returns and going down to the dungeon, fixing the brew and turning herself into the witch and so forth. These things then sort of worked together one after another as someone else is doing sequences in between, and they're tying in, because we're attending their story meetings and they're attending ours at certain times. We know what they're doing and they know what we're doing. So the continuity of the overall picture more or less blends that way, and of course Walt is in on everything. He knows what should follow.

DJ: Was it your recommendation that Art Babbitt should draw the queen or did Walt come to that? Who casted him?

BC: It would probably come from Walt.

DJ: Well, you knew Walt fairly well. Did he ever tell you why he wanted Art Babbitt to do the queen?

BC: No. Two things would cause someone to be assigned to a thing, one is the ability and the other is the availability, because sometimes someone is not available for a certain sequence. Usually it's the ability that would cast someone in then.

Interviewed in 1988 and 1990.

Dick Lundy (1909–1990)

A pioneer of personality animation, Dick Lundy is today most remembered as one of the creators of Donald Duck.

Richard James "Dick" Lundy was born in Sault Ste. Marie, Michigan, on August 14, 1907, to James and Minnie Lundy, an only child. Shortly after his birth, the family moved to Detroit where Lundy's father worked as an inspector for the Burroughs Adding Machine Company.

When Lundy was ten years old, his parents separated and he and his mother went to live in Port Huron, north of Detroit. They later moved back to the city, where Lundy's mother worked as a waitress. Lundy moved to Los Angeles in the early 1920s.

On July 27, 1929, Lundy started working for Walt Disney Productions, first assigned in the ink and paint department. In September he transferred to the animation department as an inbetweener. In March the next year Lundy was promoted to animator and later worked on *Three Little Pigs* (1933), *The Wise Little Hen* (1934), and *Orphan's Benefit* (1934). After working on *Snow White and the Seven Dwarfs* (1937), Lundy became a director at Disney.

In 1943 Lundy departed the Disney Studio and worked for Walter Lantz Productions. He started as an animator and again became a director. He directed Andy Panda, Woody Woodpecker, and the Swing Symphonies.

Lundy worked for Wolff Productions after the Lantz studio closed in 1949. Here he worked on television commercials.

In 1950 Lundy worked for MGM on Barney Bear shorts and the Droopy film *Caballero Droopy*.

In 1959 Lundy worked for Hanna-Barbera on The Flintstones, Yogi Bear, and Scooby Doo cartoons. He retired in 1973, but continued to do freelance work for several years thereafter.

Dick Lundy died April 7, 1990.

David Johnson: I would just like to know a little bit about your background, where you were born and how you came to come to the Disney Studio.

Dick Lundy: I was born in Sioux Ste. Marie, Michigan, and spent most of my [early] life in Michigan. I came out here in 1921.

DJ: Were you an art student in Michigan?

DL: Oh no, I was only 14 years old, but I did quite a bit of traveling back there. One time, my mother—mother and dad were separated—sent me from Detroit up to Warroad, Minnesota, with a tag and paper suitcase and a box of food. [Note: The 1920 census gives 1,121 souls.] That's up by the Lake of the Woods. I had four changes of trains. In Chicago, I arrived in one station and took the bus, which was a horse-drawn bus, over to another station and then had three changes besides that to get up to Warroad.

DJ: Are you Scandinavian?

DL: No. I don't know what I am. I'm Irish, English, Scotch, mongrel. And then we went from Warroad to Boudette, then to Duluth and over to Alsmirough, which was a little five-building town. The school house there had one room, first to twelfth grade. Then we went back to Detroit. Mother got hard up there and this was when I was 14 years old. Some boy friend [not in the romantic sense] of mine, his folks were moving down to Irondale, Missouri, and I went down there and stayed with them. I worked for my board and room, more or less, for six months. I was sawing. We were clearing land. We had sixty acres down there and we're just clearing it. And I see these railroad ties that sell for $9, something like that. We used to hew those out of anything above twelve inches. This was all second-growth oak, the white and black oak. He had a great big broad-axe, twelve to fourteen inches. We used to hew those square and we got 25 cents for them. But otherwise the smaller timber, why, we made mining props and that was from eight inches up. And then anything six inches up to eight we made mining ties, which were hewed up two sides. Then, the fellow I went down with, my boy friend.... It was his family , of course, but I thought he was sort of goofing off on the work, on the chores. I used to have to split the wood for the stove and I got tired of that, so I just took off one Sunday afternoon, got a job about ten miles over, for my board and room, on a farm. I didn't let them know for two weeks.

DJ: And you were still only about fourteen years old?

DL: Yeah. Meantime my mother moved from Detroit to Chicago. She got married.

DJ: You were a very independent child.

DL: I don't know. I guess so. Anyway, the whole thing was that nobody knew where I was. Finally I went back, after about two weeks, and [they] said, "Oh, your mother's frantic! Where were you?" I gave them the address and went back and stayed for a couple more weeks. My mother frantically wrote, "Hey, come on home! Come to Chicago!" I'll never forget this: as I say, I was working for my room and board and a guy took me into town. He bought me a powdered-blue hat. I had one of these motorman's haircuts, and I put this hat on and here I am arriving in Chicago with my little grip, and my mother took one look at me, "Where did you get that hat!?" She tore that off. "My gosh, let's go to the barber shop!"

She had TB and my step-dad was a registered pharmacist. So he said, "Let's go down to Albuquerque." We jumped on the train and went down to Albuquerque and he couldn't find [work] because he wasn't registered in the state. We jumped on a train and moved up to Denver and our funds were getting shorter and shorter. So we decided to walk. We were going to walk south. We started walking through the Royal Gorge and everything like that. The first night a rancher picked us up. In those days kids used knickers. When you got long pants, then you were a man. Anyway, this rancher took us in and my mother was dressed in my knickers and my socks. Here we were trudging along and this rancher came along, "Where are you going?" "Why, we're just going south." It was getting late and he said, "What are you going to do for dinner?" "We don't know." Ranches weren't too close around there. I mean, spotted around. So, he took us in, fed us that night, gave us lodging, fed us the next morning, and we started off. About noontime.... All we had was a little grip. You know what those are?

DJ: No.

DL: There're different sizes, but this one was about so high, made out of leather. It was about so long, this wide, and comes up here and then it folds in at the top. That's different than a suitcase. Suitcase was a rectangular thing. Then we had a whiskey-pint bottle for water.

We were going along there, walking away, and here's a Roe VNR G, narrow gauge, stopping for water. My stepfather said, "Let's get on that." So we climbed into an open gondola car. Here we were going around through the Rockies, there. Finally the train stopped for more water. Brakie comes up and says, "Is there a woman in this crowd?" "Yeah, my mother." And we thought, "Uh oh, we're in trouble." He says, "The conductor wants you back in the caboose." We went back there and he says, "When did you eat last?" This was in the afternoon. "We had breakfast." So he cooks us some ham and eggs and coffee. I rode up there in the cupola. This train started and was going this way. That was one of those horse-shoe bends, you know. And so they put on the brakes and my coffee went slush! He says, "Oh, I can fix that!" So he takes a piece of bread and puts it on the top of that. "That just quiets the coffee down."

We went down to Durango. And the conductor took us over to where the railroad men stayed and he paid for our dinner, paid for our lodging, paid for our breakfast and introduced us to a conductor that was going down to Farmington. Right out of Farmington was the Shiprock. It was a hundred miles of desert between Shiprock and Gallup, New Mexico. We started out across map-walking. The only thing they had to fill up our little pint bottle was sulfur water. Boy, it tasted lousy! But an old Ford touring car came along. [The driver] says, "I got room for one rider." We wanted my mother to go. She wouldn't go. So I went.

There were four trading posts across this hundred miles of desert. I went to the first one and the guy let us off. They didn't come and didn't come and didn't come. I waited until 10:30-12 o'clock. Between 10:30 and 12 o'clock, I don't remember. They put me to bed. And [my] parents showed up at 2 o'clock. They got lost. They tried to ask one of the Navajo sheep herders, and he got scared. He thought they were spirits or something, and he ran off, left his sheep. They finally found the trading post and the next morning we started out and I think the next trading post was only ten miles.

DJ: I'm not clear about one thing. You originally went to Albuquerque, New Mexico and your stepfather couldn't get a job?

DL: And then we went to Denver and he couldn't get a job.

DJ: So then you decided to go where?

DL: We didn't know.

DJ: You just wanted to go south? So you were just walking south?

DL: [My mother] had TB, so we headed south.

DJ: And now you've been walking around.

DL: Yeah. We walked to the next trading post. We were pretty low on cash. We rented a cabin there and we got up and had bought a can of beans for breakfast. Our breakfast was usually a bear-claw. It's a pastry with an icing on it. We just divide that up. Then we had coffee and we'd cook that there in the camp. Next morning we got up, had breakfast, and the sheriff was going through to Gallup. He had a prisoner. He had a seven-passenger Packard. So we ended up that night in Gallup and we got a room and [my step-dad] looked around for a job in Gallup and couldn't find one. So then he went to Flagstaff and we stayed in Gallup for a while. We stayed there for about two weeks and didn't hear from him, so we decided we were going. We had enough money to go to Flagstaff. But he had already gone down to Phoenix. So we missed him there and my mother got a job helping out in the house cleaning. I was taking care of the rabbit huts, cleaning those out. We stayed there about a week and got enough money so we went down to Phoenix and met him there. He looked around and he couldn't find a job there. Cash was getting very low by that time. I think we ended up in L.A. with six dollars. He said, "There's a freight train leaving, which connects with the main track. Let's get on it." We got on the freight train.

DJ: You didn't have to pay on the freight trains?

DL: Oh no, we were hobos. I mean, we didn't ride the rods. We just got on again in a gondola. A gondola is a box-like thing. It's not very high, the sides are only about so high. It's a flat car with sides, no top. Again we got in a gondola and rode to the junction. The train stopped and a hobo came along and said, "A few people are going west. There's a train leaving right down here." And all of a sudden we heard the toot-toots, the engines starting. They started up and as we rounded up the caboose they started to go. My mother got on first, then my stepdad. The train was going at a pretty good speed. I could run just a little bit faster. I had the rungs in my hand and I made a jump and I slipped on the step and I thought I was going to fall right under the wheels. Finally I pulled myself up and I got in. It was awfully cold, because this was in November, incidentally. And then in the mountains it starts to get cold.

So finally the train stopped again. We found an old reefer that was going back from the east, a refrigerator car. In those days they used to pack them with ice. The two ends were all boarded with slats so the cold would go thru and preserve the fruit going east but coming back they didn't bother about dumping the ice or anything, they just let it melt. There were several chunks of ice in there. We climbed down this reefer.... See, they have a hatchway for when they load it with ice. So we climbed down in there and *it was cold*. Finally the next morning a hobo again comes around. He says, "We're pulling in to San Bernardino. When this train stops it's going to go very slow when it gets into the yards. You better get off then because the railroad bulls [the detectives] are very critical. They'll arrest you for anything."

We waited till the train slowed real slow and we got off and then went over and got ourselves a motel room. The next morning we started walking into Los Angeles from San Bernardino. We walked for about an hour. We had our bear-claw for breakfast. We started walking and some guy comes along who wants to know if we want a ride. We rode right into Los Angeles. We stayed down at First and Main in L.A. We used to call them light-housekeeping rooms. What they were was sometimes one or two rooms ... sometimes a room with just an alcove where they had a stove. You could cook, and in those days they didn't have the refrigeration. Usually it was a cold box that they had out the window and you put the stuff in there and it would keep cool. That was it. I was in junior high then, eighth grade or so. Then we moved to Venice and I got into the junior high there. We moved to San Francisco when I was in the tenth grade and then we came back here 1924.

Oh, she died when I was in eleventh grade...in the spring there, March I think it was. No, it was April. So there was May, April, and June that I quit school. I never went back. I got a job in a battery shop there. When she died we had a little place out near Venice and we moved into town, Lodoro Hotel. Finally, after two weeks there my stepdad left and I never heard anything of him. I didn't know where he went and he left me with two weeks' rent. So finally I had a nervous breakdown. I had the flu or something that set me up for two weeks, and finally I went back to my old job at the battery shop. Paid off my deal. I was making ten bucks a week after school.

DJ: You went back to school then?

DL: Oh yeah. My mother [had] said, "Look, whatever you do, finish high school." That summer, a friend of mine and I went down to the ships, see if we could get a job as cabin boys.

DJ: In San Pedro?

DL: Yeah. We went down there, in San Pedro or Wilmington. It was too early in the season. The college people hadn't quite quit to go back to school. So we couldn't get a job. So I said, "Okay, then I'll go back to the battery shop."

DJ: Were you living alone at this time?

DL: Yes, at that time I was. I went back to the same hotel and they offered me a job waking people up. We had a switchboard there and I used to have to get up at 4 o'clock in the morning and every half hour why I put on ... before the people went to bed they would set an alarm for me, the first call. And I'd get up and make the calls and then go back and set the alarm for the next call. Then I would clean up the lobby. That's what I did until I graduated from high school. Except that, two months before I graduated, the hotel was sold and these people that I was living with were a bunch of gangsters. Oh, the cops wanted to talk to me. The lieutenant of the police there wanted to talk to me. He found out I wasn't connected with any of the.... But all the gangsters moved to a house and they said, "Dick, what are you going to do?" I said, "I don't know, I may have a couple more months to go to school." "Come and live with us." I said, "I can't afford it." "Who's talking money?" And they kept me.

DJ: The gangsters?

DL: The gangsters. Lot of those gangsters were killed in that massacre, you know the....

DJ: St. Valentine's Day [Massacre]. But that was in Chicago, wasn't it?

DL: Yeah, but they had moved. They were killed then. This is before.

DJ: What a story.

DL: After school let out, I went to work for $18 a week full time at the battery shop. Then a friend of the girl I was going around with had some relatives that were going up to Victoria. Would I drive their car, a Lincoln? Well, sure. The gal wanted me to wear a uniform. I said, "No way, I'm not going to wear any uniform." I drove them up to Victoria and we stayed there six months. We came back and she had a maid, but she didn't bring the maid back. She's a Canadian subject. And the maid was going to get married or something. Anyway, she wanted me to do the dusting in the house. And I didn't care for that at all.

DJ: This was your girlfriend?

DL: No, a relative of my girlfriend. In fact, she was separated from her husband—that's why she had the Lincoln. She wanted me to dust the top of the frames of the pictures and I never heard of that. That was way beyond my dealings. I finally went down in LA and got a job in a bank. Then I put in a year and a half in the bank. One of the accountants there wanted to know if I wanted to sell real estate. He said, "It's a lot more money than in the bank." I think I was making ninety-five a month.

DJ: You were only about 18 years old then?

DL: No, I was out of high school. I was nineteen, maybe twenty. I started at Disney's in 1929 so I went from real estate to Disney's.

DJ: How did that happen?

DL: A friend of mine, Les Clark [whom I had known from Venice High School who] worked on Snow White, too, was a very good animator. He got me a job at Disney's.

DJ: You've never mentioned anything about an art interest at all and yet you were an animator, so how did this...?

DL: I always drew. I mean, for Christmas presents I would get a watercolor set and I would invent my own pictures and paint them and so on and so forth. Not good.

DJ: Did you ever think or hope to have art as a career?

DL: Yes, I wanted to be a sculptor. See, [Harry] Weinbrenner was the art teacher down at Venice High, where I graduated. And he made those statues that are out in front of Venice High there. One is a statue of Myrna Loy. He was a sculptor, but he was also teaching art. In fact, he got in trouble because he wanted us to draw the live model. Well, at first we paid ten cents apiece each day, the model came in and she would pose nude there. That is unheard of in high school. One day, the model didn't show up. He said, "We'll just have to do some of these castings around here." And one gal said, "I'll pose for you." So he fixed her up. He had a flimsy deal over her breast and something down here and and we drew her. One of the teachers heard of this and they raised an awful row. That was the last of the live-art class.

I always took art. Up in San Francisco I took watercolor. I was never any good at it, but always wanted to watercolor, too. That was my art training. When I graduated, I checked in to UCLA and was going to take an art course. But at that time there was nothing as far as art went. They didn't have the art training or sessions that we had at high school. Of course, nowadays they have everything. But in those days they didn't. This was in 1926.

DJ: So you were still drawing when you were doing real estate?

DL: Oh yeah, I would. In fact, when Les made an appointment with Walt, I sat up one night doing cartoons and different things, and some stuff that I had, pen-and-ink stuff. I sort of wanted to be a pen-and-ink artist. I wasn't quite sure what I wanted to be. But sculpture-wise.... I made this character leanin5g on his elbow reading a book with his legs crossed. I looked at it and it was very rough so I threw it away and broke the head off. Weinbrenner came around and said, "Where's that statue? Where's that thing that you made?" I said, "Oh, I broke the head off and I threw it away." "You dig it out and you put that head back again." He entered it in the Crescent Bay Eisenfeld Contest, and it won second prize. Then he entered it in the Southern California [contest] and it got honorable mentions. I had it around here for a long time and I left it outside and the plaster of Paris finally got holes in it and was thrown away. I don't even think I got the ribbons that I won on the thing. So, as I say, I sat up and drew these ink sketches.

DJ: What part of the year was that?

DL: This was in the summer.

DJ: Of 1929?

DL: Yeah.

DJ: Before the big crash and stuff?

DL: Oh, yeah. So the thing is, I went over and showed Walt, and he didn't care too much for the drawings. He said, "We're having a school. Ub Iwerks is going to teach animation twice a week and if you want to attend, why fine."

DJ: What was your first impression of this man at that time?

DL: I didn't know whether he was rich, poor, or otherwise. I knew he was doing animated cartoons. He was very polite to me, of course. He was a nice guy, period. He was a genius. He didn't bounce me out or anything, but he said, "If you want to try out in the school, fine." So I did. I think it was Tuesday and Thursday was the art class by Ub Iwerks. Ub was one of the mainstays there. In fact, Ub before he left Disney, was offered.... Disney wanted to give him, I think it was, fifteen percent of the studio. But he didn't want it. He went and failed with Flip the Frog. So I said, "Okay." Tuesday I went there and I made a walk, an eight-drawing walk, shot on twos. They tested that and so Thursday when I went back, [they] said, "How do you like it?" I said, "Fine." They said, "When can you come to work?" I said, "Monday."

DJ: Were you still in real estate?

DL: I was a real estate salesman without selling anything.

DJ: Did you work on a salary, too?

DL: Yes. And they also furnished me a car. So I was stuck out, way out on 110th Street, next to where they had drilled for oil. In those days these lots would sell for $10,000 a piece because there's supposed to be oil in there, in Inglewood. But the thing was it filled with salt water just as quick as they got it in. That was the age of derricks, too. They had several of those going from here to there. This one well did come in and it was very high-grade oil. But then it got salt water in it and they couldn't do anything with it. Then, as I say, I started with Disney's the following Monday. They said, "Don't you have to give this guy notice?" I said, "I think he'll be glad to get rid of me because he's out his salary." I think I was making twenty bucks a week.

DJ: What did Walt start you with?

DL: He wanted to give me $18 [a week] and I said "I just can't live on that." He said, "Okay, make it twenty." So I started.

DJ: Five years later they were starting at $16 during the Depression.

DL: The girls were starting at $16. I started at $18 and then I got a raise.

Oh, I had a boil right there and I couldn't touch the board. So they put me out in the ink and paint department and I started inking and painting. And due to the fact that for inking I couldn't touch this arm, why, I started painting. And then I practiced the inking on cels and then finally Hazel [Sewell, head of the ink and paint department] told me … there were four girls up to here and I was sitting here, and she squeezed back and she said, "I understand you're leaving me," and I thought, "Uh oh, here I go, getting canned."

DJ: How long had you been there at this time?

DL: I think six or seven weeks. She said, "You're going in to be an assistant [animator]." So from that time on I was assistant to Burt Gillett.

DJ: This was about the time of the big crash then, because that was the end of October.

DL: By the end of the year I was making $75 a week.

DJ: Oh, you were doing real well.

DL: Yes.

DJ: Now were you frightened that the Depression might hit the studio?

DL: I didn't even know the Depression was on. I think I was making $125 a week in March 1930.

DJ: Then you must have had a cut in pay at some point?

DL: No, never did. Not until later, much later. In 1935 or 1936 I got a great big cut there. But then I had some guy stabbing me in the back. Herb Lamb was stabbing everybody he could and trying to save money.

DJ: When you became Burt Gillett's assistant….

DL: The following March, I think it was, he gave me some stuff…. He was sort of a flighty guy anyway and he gave me Mickey playing a piano. First off, he gave me keys: Mickey hit the piano like this and these keys went up and down. I had to animate those things. Then he gave me a scene by myself with just Mickey playing the piano.

DJ: What cartoon was this? Do you remember the cartoon?

DL: No, I don't. In March I actually picked up as an animator. Oh, I guess the piano was an organ, because the guy had his fanny pumping the deal. I didn't even know Walt knew that I had animated that, but evidently Burt told him about it, because they needed the animator. And Walt called me in, he said, "This is piano playing like you did on that organ scene." I said, "Oh yeah, sure." I knew enough about music. One time when I was a kid I took violin and I took that for a year and a half until I broke my wrist. I couldn't twist the thing. And a piano: I knew your upper keys were here and bass were down here. So that was it.

DJ: Did you like classical music at all?

DL: I didn't know too much about classical music. I didn't know too much about music, period. I used to dance a lot. And of course all those were bands.

DJ: You must have been a very good artist to advance so quickly.

DL: No, Walt said he hired me because I had a good line. In other words draughtsman-ship. When Freddie [Moore] started, he used to go down and look through all my surplus stuff, discards. And I said, "What are you looking at?" He was a very good artist. He said, "You do something that nobody does around here and I struggle with it. You put down in very simple language what a guy is doing. If a guy is pushing, you *know* he's pushing because you got that in your pose." And that was the thing that I seem to have: poses that I had simplified, and that was it.

DJ: You were a natural?

DL: Yeah.

DJ: What a compliment, from *him*!

DL: Oh yeah, from him. I couldn't believe it. I mean I saw him going through this and he'd pull out this paper and go through and I'd have a stack like this, then I would discard the whole thing. But he said, "Your poses are very simple." One thing led to another until *The Three Pigs*. The Three Pigs dancing in the original deal: that was mine. "Who's afraid of the Big Bad Wolf?"

DJ: You did that one?

DL: Yeah. And that was more or less copied in all the other pigs [shorts]. [Showing him a photo of the 1932 group.] This is the new one. When I went there it was a little shack in front. It had this much lawn and it only went part way back and this was an L-shaped building.

DJ: Was that also on Hyperion?

DL: Yeah. In fact he had a parking there where he built another building. Then he rented two apartments. Just before we moved [to Burbank] he had sixteen hundred employees. When I went there in 1929, there were seventeen and that included Walt, Roy, the secretary, and the janitor.

DJ: You were there when Walt thought about doing a feature-length film. Do you recall the very first time you heard about such an idea?

DL: He had thought of it for a long time, I mean, before he ever let it out. In other words, [before he] told the gang about the thing. Before these photos were taken, we used to have what they call a gag meeting. They would get up a synopsis of a story: we're going do a story about so and so.... We'd go and eat and then come back again and be there until about 9 o'clock [at night] with this circle deal.

DJ: Was this at "Ptomaine Charlie's" where you would eat?

DL: No, we wouldn't eat together. Each one of us would go home and then come back to this meeting, which started, I think, at 7 went to 9 or 9:30. It was a gag meeting. Each one would say, "How about Mickey doing this, how about Mickey doing that?" and so on. Or it was maybe a [Silly] Symphony. I worked mostly on the Symphonies.

DJ: You did?

DL: They used to have a great big head on the picture of Mickey looking right straight at you. I drew that, but Mique Nelson, the background man, painted it.

DJ: Going back to *Snow White*.

DL: I remember we were in the building that was built in back of that building there. Because I can remember I ran out of work ... [looking at a photo]. This is the building that originally was here. The soundstage and this building were built at the same time. Here's the building I'm talking about [referring to the original Hyperion building]. This was added on to here. And this [referring again to the original building] was the offices here. Ink and Paint was here, through that: this isn't a door, it's a hallway. This leads right into this door here and Ink and Paint was back there.

DJ: I want to sort of bring you back to when the announcement was made or through the grapevine you knew that something like this was going to happen.

DL: That I can't even remember.

DJ: I'll help you out. It was late in 1934 that Walt announced publicly that he would do this and there was a magazine, *Fortune*, that did an issue about the Disney empire at that time. At the very end of the article he mentions that he had just started production on *Snow White*, meaning story meetings, etc. So I know it was late 1934 when word got out. I'm just wondering what your impression was of such a revolutionary idea.

DL: I didn't have too many impressions at all there. I mean, I just went along with the deal. In other words I know that when Walt first started he said, "Now this is going to change the entire animation industry. We're going to animate differently." I started trying to think of what would be different. It finally came down to the same old animation. You had certain ways of putting things over and you did it that way. There was no change in the animation.

DJ: Except that it was better at Disney's, more beautiful.

DL: Yes, at Disney's. But then we were doing better animation than any of the other studios at that time. When dialogue first came in, why, we were doing better dialogue. I can remember in *Grasshopper and the Ants* I had the queen. And we went by inflections and accents of the track in order to animate. And this queen was talking to the grasshopper. [Sings.] That's what he played on his fiddle. And she said, "You'll change that tune when *winter* comes, when the ground is covered with *snow*." There are only two accents. And we talked from the feet on up—it wasn't like modern day [where] it's all head movement, head and mouth. Some of them don't even move the head, they just move the mouth, which is limited stuff. But we talked from the feet. [And] the inbetweener or the assistant had a dickens of a time inbetweening, because it was almost a tracing. But that queen had me stumped. I forget exactly what I did do with it. But I can remember that I would have … if I'd known what I know today, I would have used part limited animation. That would have got it over.

DJ: But they didn't do limited animation in those days.

DL: No, limited wasn't even thought of. It wasn't thought of until 1956, I think. Hanna-Barbera thought of that and I put in fourteen years with HB, so that's what it is.

DJ: How did you get involved with *Snow White*?

DL: If you had any spare time you more or less took…. The characters of the dwarfs weren't set yet. So you drew interpretations of what you thought they oughta be.

DJ: Were you present at the famous meeting when Walt called everyone in and he acted out the whole movie?

DL: I don't remember that at all. If it was a studio deal, I was in on it. [Being shown drawings of Albert Hurter.] I used to be in the same room with him. He knew all the uniforms of all the Europeans from way back. I drew a cartoon of something "Those buttons aren't right. They should be here, here. You have five here, four here." He was terrific.

DJ: Did you work on anything with him regarding *Snow White*?

DL: No. He was up there. I don't know what he was doing. They had quite a time when they moved up to the new building out in Burbank. He wanted to open a window. They said, "Look, Albert, you don't get any fresh air. The air goes out because you got fresh air inside and if you open a window you'll throw our air conditioning all off." No, no. Finally they had to bolt the damn windows shut, I think.

[Shows him drawings of layouts.] See, I worked on the dwarfs. My favorite dwarf was Grumpy. [Shows him early dwarf model sheet.] I don't know who did those. I had Sleepy or Sneezy. I had a to pose that. These were finally done by Fred Moore and he used my Sneezy or Sleepy, whatever his name was. He used my attitude in that and kept it pretty well as it was. I think it was Sneezy. I had him leaning forward….. They had a model department, you know. I tried to change one of the models for it when I was directing on one of the duck pictures. I know I got holy hell for it.

DJ: Tell me about some of the animators. Do you remember anything about Art Babbitt?

DL: Yes. Art was an extremist.

DJ: He did the queen in *Snow White*.

DL: Yeah. Art either was up here as far as quality went or he was down here. There's no half-way. The rest of the animators, they would maybe float in here and they'd have something good and then they'd have something bad. But they'd float in here. Art, no. He was down here or he was up here.

DJ: Interesting.

DL: As I say, he was an extremist. He started taking piano lessons. He takes them every day. Where you going get your practicing in? Why take piano lessons like that?

DJ: They played a joke on him. He used to have his own water.

DL: I was in on that. You could buy these little goldfish at ten-cent stores and you'd get them in a little square food carton about so high. So somebody bought one and said, "What do we do with it now? We don't want to kill it. We don't want to wash it down the drain." "Wait a minute! Is Art Babbitt here?" "No, he's still out to lunch." "Let's put them in his water bottle." We found somebody out in the parking lot to give us a signal if he comes back. So they put it down in the bottle, turned the bottle upside down and there's this goldfish swimming around. Fine. And we all went back to our rooms.

DJ: Who else was in on it besides you?

DL: Les Clark. I think Freddie Moore [and] Kimball. One other person I can't remember. We heard Art come, go into his room. We all rushed out next to the door and wanted to hear the squeal. Nothing happened. We stayed around. "Hey, something's wrong." They went in there, looked. No goldfish in the bottle. "Where did it go? I wonder if he found it and threw it away or...." He didn't find it till the next day. It had gone down into the cooler part and then came swimming back up on the thing. He found the it the next day and then he yelled. This was the joke of the whole thing. I think he threw the whole thing, the bottle of water and everything else away, and got a new deal.

DJ: What about Tytla? Did you know him?

DL: He was one of the best animators. And in *Fantasia* he had that old man on the mountain or something [Chernabog]. He was a terrific animator, he really was. He was Art Babbitt's best friend.

DJ: Tell me a little about Norman Ferguson. Did know him very well?

DL: Oh yeah. I was his assistant for a long time.

DJ: Did he ever tell you anything about *Snow White*, about how he drew the witch? Did he ever mention that to you, what kind of model he used for that?

DL: I know when we were still over in Hyperion I started in on the dance stuff. I was pretty good at dancing there, cartoon dancing. I made a dance and what I was trying to do is get this bop, bopsy-bop, all that sort of thing. What I was doing was trying to hit the accent *up*. But he's the one who said, "No, hit it *down*. Always hit an accent down." I did that and, boy, my dancing changed like that. It really got good.

DJ: This was a cartoon?

DL: Yeah.

DJ: What cartoon was that?

DL: I don't know. It's way over on Hyperion.

DJ: And Freddie Moore.

DL: I knew him very well.

DJ: And....

DL: Kimball and I started model training at the same time. We went down and measured the old low vestibule car and I drew plans for each of us.

DJ: Do you recall ever contributing one of the gags that was used in *Snow White*?

DL: No. These circles I used to tell you about that we had, the gag meetings ... so many times one fellow over here would say, "Walt, how about this?" and some [other] guy would come up and both would have the same idea. What is it that causes that? It leads you into something, your mind, and so it's the least common denominator that makes you think that way. I don't know. I mean different people writing stories will get on the same thing. This guy's on the West Coast, this guy's on the East Coast. And they get the same idea. Is it mental telepathy? That happened. I probably contributed gags, or maybe I suggested something that suggested something to him and they used his gag.

DJ: Perce Pearce stole it and told Walt it was his idea.

DL: Well, that could be. But I was never one to seek credit because I did it. If it was good, you didn't have to say, "Oh, it's tremendous, I think you're super," and stuff like that. To me that gets wishy-washy.

DJ: You don't remember anything from *Snow White* that was extremely difficult for you, that you had to labor more than you had ever done up to that point?

DL: That walk with Happy was about the biggest thing.

DJ: Because you really wanted to make it look like Happy?

DL: Yeah.

DJ: What do you think made you not figure that out while you were doing it? Because you're usually pretty bright in things like that. How did you miss that when you were doing it?

DL: We used to have these art training meetings.

DJ: Yeah, the Don Graham classes.

DL: Yeah, and we got talking about walking. We said, "[In] walking, everything moves." In other words, this goes down in a certain way and then this lifts up and this pulls this up and this does this and so on and so forth. So I drew the character. I had a good character. But when I got through with it, it was a good walk. It was one of the best walks I ever made. But it wasn't Happy. I mean, it wasn't light enough. It was a good walk, but it wasn't light. Happy is kind of heavy, but the thing was he is still light on his feet. And it wasn't that way.

DL: You went to Don Graham's classes. What did you think of them?

DL: At the start, I didn't think too much of them. At the end he got in and found out what we needed and then I liked it.

DJ: What was in the beginning that you didn't like?

DL: One thing was we had an argument there one time [about] a character falling. What happened? What hit first and what hit last and what was the reaction of that hit? And so on and so forth. And he had one deal, and I thought he was wrong, and I had another.

DJ: But he was pretty open minded, wasn't he, Don Graham?

DL: Yes, toward the end, yes.

DJ: But not in the beginning?

DL: I don't think he was. I don't think he realized *our* problem.

DJ: What about using the live models and all of that? Was that helpful for you?

DL: Not necessarily.

DJ: The anatomy classes.

DL: No, because the first thing you knew … I was starting to put shapes on the arms when they didn't have shapes.

DJ: Oh, so you were way ahead of your time, then.

DL: The thing was that I would go to draw an arm [and] the first thing you know I had a muscle here and a muscle here and … hey, wait a minute! I didn't know that much about muscles. So it was throwing me off. I didn't go back to the old rubber hose [style]. I had an elbow where an elbow should be. But the thing was that I started putting in shapes there and then. You don't want that.

DJ: So the anatomy lessons were more hindering to you….

DL: Yes.

DJ: What about these movies that Walt had everyone go see. He would rent a theater and he would have everyone come down to watch these nature films and there were art films from Europe. Do you remember those things?

DL: Not too well. I used to go to them. I know that. Because if Walt said go, you went.

DL: Because those aren't mentioned too often.

DL: I know one time, we had a professor from Harvard, I think. I forget his name. And he was supposed to study us and find out what was wrong with us.

DJ: What was wrong with you?

DL: What we could do to improve our viewpoint or whatever it was. Then finally, the day he's going to leave, Walt rents a theater and we all go down there and [the professor] praises us to the sky. He says, "Your outfit is really tops in my estimation. You don't argue about … you don't have these differences. There's no jealousies."

DJ: There were jealousies.

DL: There were, yeah. There were jealousies, but not the way he meant them. Even if you were jealous of [someone], if he had something you could use, why you went in and tried to get it. [Bill] Roberts was one guy that I could never get anything out of. He'd always say, "It's something like this ... I don't know ... you can figure it out for yourself." In other words, "What did you put into it that gave it that effect?" He would never tell you.

DJ: Maybe he didn't know.

DL: Maybe not, but it was more or less as if you were bothering him, and his time. You always had time to fool around, because you had time to think. A lot of times.... I couldn't sit down at the board all day long and just animate. I had to visualize exactly what I was going to do. Once I got it in my mind, I could do it. But until I got it in my mind, I couldn't.

DJ: Would you sometimes look out the window and get ideas.

DL: Yes, I would look out the window, but I probably wouldn't see anything. Or I might even turn to a magazine and flip the pages of a magazine. But I wouldn't look at the magazine. Lot of times, I would get it at night. I would wake up in the morning and I'd have it.

DJ: Would you say that sometimes you would sit and hardly draw during the whole day because you didn't have any ideas? Did that ever happen?

DL: Yes. Not the whole day. But usually what I would do if I got really stuck on something, I'd put it aside and go on to something else. Because we wouldn't pick up one scene at a time, we picked up a sequence. Or it might strike you, or you might say, "I'll try this." And then, after you got through, you'd flip the thing. "No, that isn't it, what is it? How will I put this over?" I mean you go through all the things.... What do you have to do to put something over? One thing is silhouette. You silhouette something. You never pick up something and hold it right in front of you like this [close to you]. It's out here. If you want to look at something, you have the character look at it, see. So you go over all of those things. What is it? Like one time I animated a scene and the layout man put the thumbs on the wrong side of the hand. The palm was this way but the thumb was down here. I animated that whole scene, but at the end I had to have the thumbs like this. And I went back to the layout man and that's the way he had it. But I didn't notice it.

DJ: Did he want it like this?

DL: No, no. He just put it on the wrong side.

DL: So you never even realized.

DL: I didn't realize they went through the whole scene, this. A stack of drawings about so thick. I changed the whole thing so that....

DJ: Do you recall if any of the Hollywood actors, famous actors, influenced you when you did the dwarfs. Any particular piece of business or anything like that?

DL: No. I can't recall.

DJ: Any outside influence?

DL: No, the preconception is a sleepy person is one way, a sneezy person ... that's the way I thought of it. If you've got a cloud and it's grumpy, what do you do? You frown, and you're belligerent. So everything is that way, your timing is that way.

Interviewed on January 26, 1990.

Grim Natwick (1890-1990)

Myron H. "Grim" Natwick was born on August 16, 1890, in Centralia, Wisconsin. During his impressive career, which started around 1916 and lasted till 1977 when he collaborated on the feature *Raggedy Ann and Andy*, Grim Natwick worked with virtually all the legends of animation: Max and Dave Fleischer, John Terry, Ub Iwerks, Chuck Jones, Richard Williams, and of course, Walt Disney.

Having attended the Art Institute of Chicago, he was one of the first animators to be classically trained in the arts.

His adventure in animation began in 1916 when he joined the Hearst-owned IFS studio. Natwick then moved to Max and Dave Fleischer, where he created Betty Boop in 1930. In the early 1930s he joined Ub Iwerks' Celebrity Productions where he redesigned the Willie Whopper character to give him more personality.

On November 12, 1934, Natwick was hired by the Disney Studio, where he supervised the cookie heroine in *The Cookie Carnival* (1935), the violin princess in *Music Land* (1935), and the blind doll in *Broken Toys* (1935). His biggest "role," however, was Snow White herself, which he animated along with Ham Luske.

Natwick left the Disney Studio in 1938 (the last project he tackled there being the short *Mother Goose Goes Hollywood*) to work on Fleischer's *Gulliver's Travels* and *Mr. Bug Goes to Town*, then joined Walter Lantz in 1944 to animate Woody Woodpecker. In the 1950s he could be found at UPA in New York, working on Mr. Magoo. Although he officially retired in 1968, he joined Richard Williams five years later to help train the animators of *The Thief and the Cobbler*, and then returned to animating for the last time, on the movie *Raggedy Ann and Andy*.

Grim Natwick died Sunday, October 7, 1990.

David Johnson: I want to ask you about *Snow White*.

Grim Natwick: *Snow White* was a major, major achievement, even by today's standards. When you begin to compare it with other pictures it's simply remarkable that it holds up. Of course, no other [cartoon] picture had quite this much planning. I know Walt was planning this thing two or three years before he actually made it. And at that time he had undoubtedly the greatest staff of animators that were ever brought together, and they were all groomed just for this one picture. It was pretty hard, being the first animated feature. There's nothing to compare it with. At that time I think it was the only picture that crowded *Gone with the Wind*. I believe that it was the biggest money-making picture. Am I right on that?

DJ: It was the biggest until *Gone With The Wind*.

GN: Oh, that was it. Did you have feelings about certain characters that could have been better done?

DJ: Quite the contrary. In some ways, I think it's never been equaled—certainly never surpassed—never will be. But, as a matter of fact, what interests me is how and when you first came to the studio and were they already working on *Snow White* [at the time]?

GN: In 1930, I was working for the Fleischer Studio in New York, and I had previously worked in about two or three studios. I knew the crowd at the Felix the Cat studio back in New York: Bill Nolan and Otto Messmer. Anyway, I had worked on Krazy Kat with Bill Nolan. Back in those student days the studio had about twelve people, or something like that. And of course, to back up a little, it was in 1930 that I created Betty Boop and instantly Walt Disney offered me a job and every other studio in Hollywood. Every one of them had been trying to create a girl character and couldn't do it. Drawing a girl is different from Mickey Mouse or Minnie Mouse or Bugs Bunny or things that are funny little characters. Snow White had to be almost a real character and the reason was very simple: I had about eight years of art school experience and most of these kids had maybe a year or two at one of the smaller schools.

DJ: Didn't you study in Europe?

GN: I studied over there three years.

DJ: Where?

GN: In Vienna. I wanted to be an illustrator. They were the aristo-crats of the art world at that time: not because they were always the greatest artists, but they were the best paid artists. I coincidentally have worked with one of them, Dean Cornwell, in a commercial art studio in Chicago. I was just an art school kid, but he had come up from Kentucky and he wasn't a rich guy, but he was good enough to earn a good living, and he happened to be working in a commercial art studio where I was learning to letter. I had just come out of a little town, up in Wisconsin, went to art school and had about three jobs, one of them was as a supernumerary. One of the kids in the art schools was smart enough to.... I don't know how he got the job, but he dug up supernumeraries for the theaters, for the shows: if they need six soldiers to wear iron uniforms or something. You didn't have to do any talking. Why, we got about a dollar a night for taking those parts. And, of course, all the kids I knew had a restaurant job, [so] there'd be a couple of [free] meals. And then I had another job where I worked for a friend of the family who sold school books, and I could run in on Saturdays or even Sundays and help him to fix boxes up and do something. Once in a while he'd send me out on an errand to a little country school in Illinois or Wisconsin or somewhere. So I'd picked up enough change to gradually get along, particularly this job in the Art Service, and this commercial artist—funny, he came from a little town right near where I'm living in Missouri now mostly—taught me how to letter and then we did a lot of commercial lettering jobs. Most of their work was like this post office [stuff], a little advertise-ment on it, a post card or something, but there's always a lot of fancy letters. And this man's tobacco store got a real bargain.

I had met a kid up in my home town who was fairly brilliant. I should back up. In those days there was no radio, there was no television, and the phonograph was quite new, and everybody had an organ or a piano, and somebody in the family would learn how to play it and the rest of the family would come in and sing. They entertained themselves. So many stores, like Woolworth's, would have a song counter almost the length of this room, and a professional piano player who had some kind of a voice, and these shop girls would come in and look over the rolls of song, and if they liked the title and the picture that was on it they'd ask him to sing it, so that they would see whether they liked it. After I had worked with this letter artist a year or so and learned a little about it, a kid in my home town had written a song. Every small town has one or two brilliant musicians who may be young or any age ... but this kid that'd written this song ... there were song publishers who specialized in that and so that's what happened to him. He got this song printed and he asked me if I would design the cover. Of course, I wasn't a skilled artist, so I just sort of borrowed a thing: a pretty girl head from Gibson. I don't know if you ever heard of the Gibson Girls?

DJ: Oh yes.

GN: He was a millionaire artist who was so famous that his drawings were in the Louvre. He was the greatest pen-and-ink artist who ever lived in the world probably, particularly in the human character. So I put the lettering on it and maybe this boss helped me with it, I don't remember. Chicago was filled with song publishers, many of them branches of New York publishers. I took this song cover down to Bob Graham, or something like that. I showed it to him and asked him if he could use any of my art, and he did. He said, "Gosh, yeah, that's pretty good, we could use it." To many of the song-cover artists it was not a steady business, but he handed me a song to do and I took it. Of course, the artist I was working with brightened up my lettering a little bit, but all of a sudden I had a printed sample of a song cover that I could take to other publishers. So very soon, golly, I was able to earn a living. All in all, over a period of the next two or three or four years, I probably did two hundred song covers. I did all of W.C. Handy's, starting with "St. Louis Blues." Blues had just [come in]. Eventually, instead of going from studio to studio and picking up jobs I met a printer of music and he handled all of the amateur things that came from every state in the Union, like this kid from my home town. So eventually I met a publisher who printed the music and the song and the cover. He would take the whole job for about $60 in those days, and if they didn't have an artist to do the cover, why he'd find one. If they didn't have a writer to write the words, he'd find one. And funny, some of the pros picked up a little extra change by just ... I mean people who were writing theatrical productions would work for him, and so some of those songs, if the music was good, and everything else [could make a little extra]. So he put me in a room in the center of Chicago and I did all the covers. That gave me steady income. I didn't have to work anymore for this [letter outfit].

DJ: Did you go to Vienna after that?

GN: Yes, ten or fifteen years after. But in Chicago I met this one illustrator, Dean Cornwall. I don't know if you know the names of the illustrators.

DJ: I know Leyendecker.

GN: Leyendecker, yeah. There were two of them. They were cover designers primarily for the *Saturday Evening Post* and other magazines. They were the fellows who earned two thousand bucks a week, or something like that. I saw an ad in a newspaper a couple of weeks ago asking for original paintings by those artists like Norman Rockwell and people like that. And now those things that the *Saturday Evening Post* paid twenty-five hundred dollars a cover—which was a terrific lot—that was a year's salary for some people—they are now selling for more than $100,000 and they're trying to find them, because there'll never be another period [like that again].

DJ: Just like the Disney cels from *Snow White*.

GN: That's right. I remember when they [released] *Snow White*. There was a table about as long as from here to the wall [approximately twelve feet] and a girl in the front office phoned everybody and said, "The drawings we're no longer using on *Snow White* are piled up on a table downstairs. You may help yourselves." I imagine that that pile of drawings—they were this high on the table—they probably would be worth today a quarter of a million dollars.

DJ: Probably more. Did you or do you own a lot of your own drawings?

GN: I had a sale and made a few thousand bucks a couple of years ago.

DJ: Who did you sell them to?

GN: They were auctioned off in New York [by Christie's].

DJ: What year did you finally get to the Disney Studio?

GN: In 1930 I created Betty Boop. I worked for so many studios. I first worked for William Randolph Hearst in the 1920s. I went to New York and got into this song publishing artwork very deeply. I was doing all these songs, but that was during the war. Everybody in America wrote a song about how we hated the Kaiser and how we were going over to beat him up. I was turning out a song cover a day for HS Talbot who printed them up, and then I got drafted into the army myself in World War I. That took me out of the thing for a while, and when the war ended I went to New York. In 1930 I had just got back from studying over in Vienna and still wanted to be an illustrator but earn enough money so that I could afford to get started, I worked for Fleischer's [and shortly after created Betty Boop]. And the offers from Hollywood—gosh—Roy Disney took me out to dinner five nights in a row and came up to my studio and we watched the Rose Bowl game ... no, we *listened* to it on the radio ... still no television. And he told me all the reasons why I should come out to Walt's. The main reason was that there was only one other man in the animation business who could draw a girl character, let alone animate her, and Walt Disney was already starting to work on *Snow White*. [Note: Work on *Snow White* did not begin until 1934.]

DJ: Now you were in the east when Roy Disney came out to....

GN: Yes, I was working for Fleischer.

DJ: And that's when Roy Disney came out and said Walt wanted you.

GN: That's right. But I had so many offers, I could work at any studio. So I decided to work for [Ub] Iwerks. It had to be about 1935 when I came out here [to Walt's]. In that period [1932], I came out and worked for Iwerks, because at that time everybody thought that Iwerks was the brilliant studio. Walt was just a businessman, which wasn't true, but that's from three thousand miles away. Walt had stopped animating, but he was a pretty good artist, actually, and in his books where are printed a few of his drawings he wasn't a bad artist. But Iwerks was the brilliant creative artist. He created [*i.e.*, he drew the character of] Mickey Mouse. But really I chose Iwerks because he offered me the most money. [Laughs] So gradually I became an unofficial supervisor, director I guess you'd call it. They didn't have names for them. I was probably the oldest by a number of years at the Iwerks Studio, and he had a lot of young artists.

DJ: Would you say you got to Disney's about 1935?

GN: I would say about then. [Note: Natwick joined Disney on November 12, 1934.] I probably worked for Iwerks a couple of years.

DJ: When you first came to the studio, were you working with Ham Luske, who was designing [the character of] Snow White?

GN: Ham Luske was the other animator on [the character of] Snow White and [he had a great reputation], while I was there anyway. I knew Ham very well. Of course the studio wasn't that big, and we had lunch with these guys every day. Ham was the other animator who could animate a girl and he had this famous.... Who was the Milwaukee singer that became very famous? A rather hefty gal. She was quite filled out but a little risqué. She made quite a few Hollywood pictures. Ham Luske animated her in *Who Killed Cock Robin?*

DJ: Oh, Mae West.

GN: Mae West. And so Ham was the only artist that Walt was sure could draw a girl. All these guys were brilliant at comic characters, but most of them had never gone to art school. They started out with some artists who learned to draw a cartoon character, and I was very [skilled] because I wanted to be an illustrator and I knew I had to be able to paint a girl character, because illustration has stories usually of boy/girl themes.

DJ: When you first came to the studio, did you work with Ham Luske on the character of Snow White?

GN: No, that picture was not being done yet. I may have been there a year [before I started on Snow White]. At first, they didn't have a picture ready to be put into animation. Actually Ub Iwerks had offered me half of [his] studio if I would stay with him, but we were getting rumors then that Walt was working on a feature picture and I decided that I wanted to work on it, the first feature picture ever animated. Before I got to Disney's, actually, there were fifteen ex-New Yorkers who had come out to work at Disney's, like Ted Sears. Ted Sears was the primary storyman at the Disney Studio and I had palled around with him more or less out in New York. So every Friday night we'd get together and see the amateur prize fights: a group of ex-soldiers. The American Legion had a big building and they'd have prize fights there, semi-professional fights. There was a rumor that was pretty prevalent that if you had ever been offered a job by Walt Disney and turned him down he'd never offer you another job. Ted, I knew, rated very high with Walt, so I made up my mind that I'd like to work on *Snow White*, and by that time they were beginning to storyboard it and pick out ... they had, I think, four groups of directors and divided the picture [between] them, and each group had three or four men on it. *Snow White* was going into the works by this time. I said to Ted one night at dinner, "If you ever see Walt in a good mood, you might mention me and say you understand Grim would like to work on *Snow White* and give me a chance to do it." A couple of weeks [later] he called me up and said, "Walt will talk to you Friday night after work." It didn't take me long to get down there. It was an interesting meeting. Walt, apparently, was all alone. He spent most of this time showing me around the studio. They were very proud of it. He stopped in on a couple of animators and showed me what they were doing—working on Mickey—particularly an animator who finished his work beautifully. I was always kind of a slapstick man. I liked to rough things out quickly and roughly. But this guy was a brilliant clean-up man [Dick Huemer]. He had worked for Fleischer's and many of his drawings are in the Fleischer book. I thought, "Christ, if I have to draw like this...." I'd been knocking out Flip the Frog and stretching him and flattening him out and doing things with him, but, golly, it pretty near scared me, actually. But I thought I would risk it.

DJ: Was there any artwork for *Snow White*—storyboards that he showed you?

GN: I didn't see a thing at that time. He didn't even mention *Snow White*. He just showed me the studio and what a beautiful men's wash room they had. [Laughs] Then we agreed on a salary. I didn't think it was the time to start arguing with Walt. Next Monday I was working for him.

DJ: Do you remember how much you were being paid at that time?

GN: I was paid one hundred fifty bucks a week.

DJ: By Walt?

GN: Uh huh.

DJ: That's a lot of money in those days.

GN: Oh yeah, it is a lot of money in those days. Iwerks had paid me two hundred.

DJ: Oh, I see.

GN: But Iwerks, when he found the studio could go and get along, he left the whole thing in my hands, I mean the hard part of it, so I suppose that I earned the money. It was, at that time, a pile of money.

DJ: What do you remember about *Snow White*? The first things that you can recall?

GN: There were many meetings before they ever got into animation. But the first meeting they had [that I attended], Walt called in all of the animators. I would say all who would work on it. Probably there were some animators that continued with the shorts for a while and particularly the directors. You might say that Walt had, I believe, four director groups.

DJ: I think there were five. Bill Cottrell, Ben Sharpsteen, Larry Morey, Will Jackson, and Perce Pearce.

GN: There were probably dozens of meetings before they called in the animators. But this time they gave us a summing up of what it was and they asked us all to submit drawings. They kind of gave us a synopsis of the plot and said to throw in any drawings you can think of that might be used anywhere … fit in any of the gags. They didn't bring up many of the gags there, but they gave you a quick list of the different periods in the picture. I grew up in a small town on the Wisconsin River. In summer we'd spend about half of our time in the river and about half out, sitting in the sun. I remember when the water lowered in the river, the paper mill…. They had to clean out the mill during the summer and they'd take out these dams and the river was lowered down, and in the bottom of the river were great big rocks, some as big as this room. The soft-shell turtles would climb up and sun themselves. I thought, "A turtle is an interesting character." We always had one in our pants pocket when we were kids, a frog or a turtle or something. So I made a lot of sketches of turtles doing different things, and they made a lot of use of it. I didn't give them any gags. I don't remember what I drew, but they wrote it in right into the story and used him for a scrub board and used a gag of him. He was still going up the stairs when they started running down and he toppled over and skidded out of the house.

DJ: So you contributed a turtle to the story?

GN: Yeah. … They did ask us for gags to be submitted. I used to pick up five or ten bucks every once in a while, and I guess Walt worried about the animators wasting too much time. It probably cost him more than ten bucks for the gag. They had one of my gags—a fifty-dollar gag—in the story right up to the last week. I used to lunch with the storymen because Ted Sears was top storyman around there on the shorts so we had lunch every day. They told me that my gag was in the $50 bracket.

What was it? Somebody had to get up to the top-story window. I guess somebody was up there and the house was fire or something.

DJ: Oh, this wasn't in *Snow White*?

GN: Oh no, this was just a short. I think that the giraffe happened to saunter across at that time, something like that, and [I] used him for a ladder. But they came up with something else at the last minute and I [never got the fifty bucks].

DJ: So you were in on some of the early story meetings on *Snow White*, before they actually started the animation?

GN: Yeah. They had a pile of stuff that high, and they didn't sort it out.

DJ: I read that for several months you did experimental animation on the girl. Do you remember anything about that?

GN: Yes. Very few artists pretended to draw a girl, but there may have been four or five of them. And a couple of my drawings were shown in [*Look*] magazine, last May.

DJ: I understand that Walter Lantz was called in as a consultant on *Snow White* in the very early stages.

GN: I never heard of that. But it's possible because Walt's experience in Hollywood exceeded Walter Lantz's at that time. I met Walt when I was working on Krazy Kat. Him and his brother Roy, when they'd come east, they would visit the other studios. He may have wanted to persuade Bill Nolan to come out.

DJ: You said you drew Snow White as a little princess.

GN: Yes, with a three-pointed crown. I may not have thought of the story where she was in rags. Later on, however, I designed the dress that she wore in rags, because I got that scene and they didn't have a costume. [I show him a model sheet of Snow White in Natwick's rag costume, drawn by his assistant Marc Davis.] Yes, I think one of the faults is a lot of artists who deserve credit didn't receive any. Marc was a brilliant artist and he cleaned up my animation.

DJ: Do you remember some of the experimental work you did on *Snow White*?

GN: Of all the animators that worked on her, I think Ham and I are the only premiere animators....

DJ: And Jack Campbell.

GN: He was my assistant.

DJ: Was he? Because he was given many big scenes to do for the picture.

GN: Yes. Jack wanted a chance to animate and so he came to me. He may have talked to Ham earlier, but up to this time we really had no girls to animate. Then he had cleaned-up maybe three or four of my scenes. The first scene Walt gave us, he said, "Take a whole month on this one scene. Just [take your time]. Everything you find that doesn't work tell us and we'll change it."

DJ: What scene was it?

GN: I've forgotten. I did eighty scenes in the picture. He gave us a whole month, and we didn't ever have to submit one inch of animation to go into the picture. We could work them over or do anything we wanted to. I've forgotten what that first scene was.

When they decided on the costume she would have, they had twenty-five story meetings on it. They decided as long as she was to be in this costume most of the picture that [it should be one which] most of the inbetweeners could draw. Mine may have been a little too sophisticated.

DJ: Did you work with Luske in the same room?

GN: No.

DJ: And Jack Campbell was originally your assistant?

GN: Yes. He wanted to animate and I wouldn't attempt to stop him. I could have complained to Walt but I wouldn't. I think Marc was a better artist, from my point of view, although Campbell had years of experience. Yeah, Jack worked for me until we got onto *Snow White* and I never, ever thought of trying to hold anyone back. I don't know what Walt would have said if [he knew how Jack felt about animating the girl] and I wouldn't be curious to find out. Because Jack and I used to bowl together and do everything else together. We were pretty close friends.

DJ: You don't recall any conflict between you and Ham over the character of Snow White?

GN: I don't recall. I was never one to hold back my opinion, but so far as I know there was never any conflict between Ham and myself because I admired him. If I remember right, I went to a party at the Disney Studio ... and that was years later when I was working with UPA. And gosh, they had a long bar and I came up to order a drink and Ham was there and he reached over and gave me a terrific handshake. I guess he respected me as much as I did him, because we both knew that most of the Mickey Mouse animators couldn't even draw Snow White. Because it isn't even drawing a girl. There's something about the line itself. A feminine line is different than a masculine line. There're different kinds of lines in drawings. Drawing a nude man and a nude woman, it's like switching to Mickey Mouse or something from a photograph.

DJ: So you felt the line should be feminine looking?

GN: All of the subtleties. You've got to know what the muscles are underneath the skin. You've got to retain a feeling of subtleness. A woman doesn't walk like a man. Yes, I was glad that I had had eight years of art school. And that was over a period of about twenty years.

DJ: The classes given by Don Graham ... did you go to any?

GN: Yes.

DJ: Do you remember anything about those?

GN: I went because I enjoyed drawing from a live model, just as long as you have a model hired by somebody else. [Laughs] Walt wanted everybody to learn how to draw better and always hoped, I guess, that he could have been in there doing the drawing himself.

DJ: I know you've talked a lot in the past about how you didn't like to use the rotoscope, but didn't the rotoscope help with the timing, for instance?

GN: We changed it often. We never went in and told Walt we were doing it. [Here he talks about the one-hundred-and-one rotoscoped images of one particular scene from *Snow White*—the scene of Snow White immediately prior to her running down the stairs after hearing the pot boiling over, which was partly cut in the final version—and how he used the first and last ones but everything in between was done free hand, without the rotoscope. He never told this to Walt, who upon seeing it, is said to have stated, "That's just what I want!"] And we took liberties. Walt never said, "Don't do this," but if it didn't work, you got the scene back and re-animated it.

DJ: Do you recall any scenes from *Snow White* you did that you had to re-animate?

GN: In the early, preliminary scenes I think we animated three of one.... Marc Davis was with me at the time. Actually what happened, I believe, was they never got into the picture. He gave us a practice scene that wasn't even in the story, but they were written out or something.

DJ: You don't remember what that was, do you?

GN: No. The first three or four scenes we got were pretty simple scenes. Like her running across the room, picking up something. The little scene may have been seven or eight feet. Of the last twenty scenes I cannot remember one that came back for changes.

DJ: But the early scenes you were talking about, they were just for experimental....

GN: I think that Walt was satisfied with them and figured, "This is safe. We can go ahead."

DJ: Do you recall looking at the live action through the moviola?

GN: Oh yes. Marc and I each had one. We had [Lester] Novros work with us. We were kind of a three-step sort of thing. And late in the picture when we were trying to finish it up, a couple of other kids ... they were very good assistants. Oh, Tony Rivera, a very good artist, cleaned up some of my drawings later, toward the end, to finish up the picture, to get it on the road.

DJ: Milt Kahl?

GN: Milt did the prince in some of the scenes. Milt had no experience [at animating the human figure], but he was a terrific artist. Later on, of course, Milt was doing all the animation. He became a marvelous animator. Milt's early animation was fastidiously and perfectly done, but he traced it too close to the photographic tracings. What I did on one scene, I remember, when [the prince] was walking over to sing under the window, I suggested throwing a couple of trees in the foreground so that you wouldn't be conscious of the walk. I don't think I ever took a scene back. I may have corrected a drawing or two or three or something. I wanted these fellows to do the thing as well as I could do it. The particularly tough part of the thing, of course, I would fill in, leaving only simple inbetweens. Things like a walk, normally, you'd take for granted. But take an [inexperienced] guy like Milt and expect him to do *anything* in the picture was extraordinary. He very quickly became one of the real great animators at the Disney Studio. Remember these kids came in because primarily they drew exceptionally well, and I never corrected anything that I thought would work.

DJ: What scenes did you particularly enjoy when you saw it last time?

GN: The whole series where she is picking flowers and the hunter comes in. I think in some ways that was the most successful scene.

DJ: [Showing him pictures of Snow White dancing with the dwarfs I asked him if this would have been particularly difficult. This was actually done by both Natwick and Campbell.]

GN: No, this was really one of the easier scenes to do, because it was moving so much we could use lots of rotoscope. For that reason it was on the close-up stuff that we had to be very careful of her eyes, nose, and lips, and what happened [to those things]. I was pretty well pleased with most of these scenes, because the skirt was moving and it was at a fast tempo.

DJ: So the faster the scenes, the easier it was?

GN: Ordinarily, they could not pinpoint a defect.

DJ: It was a beautiful scene.

GN: I thought it was a very fortunate scene.

DJ: In some of the scenes you did, one can see the similarity in your drawing and the original model for Snow White, Marge Belcher. Was that intentional?

GN: No. But [after] eight years in art school, I may have sensed certain things that the assistant would not. I had a terrific pair of eyes at that time.

DJ: Were there any scenes that were particularly difficult that you had to work hard at more than the others?

GN: The ones where she was moving more slowly. I received one scene and there were, I think, one-hundred-and-one drawings. I used [number] one and one hundred and one [of the rotoscoped images]. Because she was singing "Some Day My Prince Will Come" I believe. [Here Natwick is apparently confusing this with the scene discussed earlier, on page 64.] You can imagine "Some Day My Prince Will Come." So I just threw them all out [the rotoscopes] and animated the whole thing [free hand] because I was sure that it would jitter if I had used those drawings. Now it's very possible that in photographing it they were unaware that she almost sat still at that time.

I know in one case while she was staying pretty still in one mood, I deliberately [asked the director that the camera] panned over to one of the dwarfs, because the rotoscope would have been monotonous to see her in that almost one, still, position. We were given total liberty to do what we wanted to, and every time I felt if it would do better to pan over to a dwarf clapping his hands or something and then come back to Snow White [we would do it]. The animation [is pretty much set by] the animators, the [directing animator], once he gets those rotoscope drawings, and nobody ever jumped on us for any mistakes we made. So I guess most of it looked all right to Walt.

DJ: Do you remember being nervous in a sweat box session with Walt?

GN: I can't recall one. In fact, I never was nervous because when I was working for Walt I was offered jobs about every month or so....

DJ: I don't mean nervous about getting fired.

GN: Oh, nervous about *my* work? Some of them were very tough. Some we had to take liberties with.

DJ: Can you recall which ones?

GN: Not off hand. I'd have to go through the picture. [Here I show him photos and reprints from the movie, one with Snow White telling Grumpy to wash. "Yes, that's my scene." And when she's kissing Grumpy: "Oh yes, and I think I animated Grumpy there, where he gets his nose stuck in a tree. I feel very sensitive about that. I recall it. But maybe I didn't."]

DJ: Bill Tytla did Grumpy.

GN: Oh yes, I remember talking to Bill about some of the scenes.

DJ: Oh, you did?

GN: That one, because for two years I had a room next to Bill and we became very close. Bill and Art Babbitt lived together at that time.

DJ: And all of this was easy for you to do?

GN: The drawing was an awful lot of fun. But to get the spacing and the timing and the picture, how many frames would that be held so the audience would get it... The timing of it [was more challenging]. The rotoscope, of course, gave you a great deal of help. But it didn't give you the psychology of the thing. And we had to put in the accents.

DJ: Can you talk more about what you just said?

GN: I guess it just comes down to a sense of directing. This was after twenty years or so [of drawing]. I hadn't been in animation all that time but gone to art school and drawing.... But you want to be sure that the audience knows what's happening. Much of the commercial stuff, for example, the timing is *way* off. You get a picture of a character and then they do something and you don't exactly know what they did. I remember, I had an experience—I won't mention the director's name—but when I first worked at Walt's, they didn't have any animation for a week or two. I cleaned-up and made color drawings of the different models and characters that were used.

DJ: In *Snow White*?

GN: Not in *Snow White*. But on *Cookie Carnival* . I drew or re-drew the head drawings of some of them. I polished them up. Like the hair on the Cookie Queen was whipped cream or something. And later on I animated some of these so I felt that I knew the character before I ever got them. I was thinking of another case. One of the early pictures I worked on, I believe. It was *Mickey's Fire Brigade* and Mickey Mouse was a fireman and he fell through the roof of a house and landed in a bathtub [with] Clarabelle Cow who was in there. Now I always wanted to make sure that the audience knew what happened before he got a response.

Anyway, I'd animated this thing, Mickey fell in in a splash. Now I wanted to be sure that the splash was out of the way. The water dripped out of his eyes and *then suddenly* he realized he's in a bathtub with a naked cow and he's very, very surprised. But Ben [Sharpsteen] whittled it down, so he's surprised as soon as he landed. It wasn't very long before one day Walt's secretary called me up and said, "Walt would like to talk to you after work." And so, after work, I walked in and Walt was sitting behind a big, long table with all [different] scenes and drawings [on it] and telephones and everything else, and he reached down and got a box of cigars and he said, "Do you smoke cigars, Grim?" All of us, animators, quite a few of us smoked cigars. Cigarettes would go out too quickly. You'd be making a drawing and a cigar would still be lit afterwards. So he lighted a cigar and I sat down on the divan about a third longer than that one [points to a six-foot divan] and he went back and picked up a stack of cards and flipped through them and said, "Some nice things have been said about you, Grim." Then I forgot how he wandered off in the end of a sentence and he said, "Is there anything you'd like to say yourself?" I didn't want to blackball Sharpsteen, because we worked together in New York and his desk was next to mine [at the time]. I said, "Walt, I don't think.... I'm kind of a slapstick animator. I like the psychology of animation, and I feel in some cases that Ben's changed my drawings. In fact, I don't think you are getting *my* animation." And we had quite a long chat there, me trying to avoid knocking Sharpsteen. Walt said: "Do you think you'd do better with another director?" I said I didn't think it would hurt any. I didn't think it would be any worse. The next director I got in with.... [The short was] called *Alpine Climbers*. Who directed that?

DJ: Dave Hand.

GN: Yeah, Dave Hand. There were some real tough scenes in there. As a matter of fact, one of them that I animated of Mickey trying to steal eagle eggs ... there was a little scrap between Mickey and the eagles.... They used that as a test scene for animators who came out from the East. They had them re-animate that to see how good it was. On that particular picture not one drawing was changed, not *one tiny thing* was changed. Nothing in the picture was changed and I got a $500 bonus on that one. That was my answer to Sharpsteen. Not once in the next four years that I was there did Walt ever say a word to me about my animation. [This was not entirely true. Virtually everyone at Disney's (not only animators) at this time was subjected to memos criticizing their work and how to improve it. Grim was no exception.]

DJ: You said there were tough scenes in *Alpine Climbers*. Were there any tough scenes in *Snow White*?

GN: The main toughness is to be sure the eyes are lined up, that the nose doesn't get too big, or that the lips get out of place a sixteenth or a sixtieth of an inch. You've got a blank face there where you have to be very, very careful. The inbetweens had to be watched very carefully unless it was fast action. For Snow White, you had to know how to animate, to really get the timing, because sometimes there's a stuttering in the movement or the tracing of lines are bad. You've got to be sure that the flow of the dress was always a natural flow. We discarded many drawings because we felt that it slowed it up a little bit, and we could get what we wanted in by putting in a couple of our own inbetweens somewhere else. We re-timed quite a lot of that as well, of the same thing as the splash in the bathtub. I think that Sharpsteen put it in too soon [Mickey's surprise]. He lost the psychology of the scene. The thing an animator can do *pre-eminently* is to psyche an audience if they know how to time it. If they can't feel it, they can't do it.

DJ: So for *Snow White*, you re-timed some of the director's timings? Is that what you're saying?

GN: Well, it was only photographed and it moved, and gave its position. But, yeah, like that one scene of one hundred drawings: I forget whether I re-timed that completely or whether I cut away from it a little quicker and cut to the dwarfs or something. We had total privilege, which we used, of re-timing any of that. I didn't like any of my animation in *Fire Brigade*, because Sharpsteen had re-timed everything. He kept changing things and changing things. Now that might have been all right for these kids that were learning how but, boy, it was a pretty bad start and I'd been in animation for six or eight years, probably longer than Sharpsteen had.

DJ: Did you notice that when you were doing Snow White from the live-action rotoscope, you had to exaggerate a lot of the motion?

GN: Oh, you exaggerate anytime you are photographing, or have it done over.

DJ: The rotoscope was re-photographed, you mean?

GN: I think if they ran it and it didn't look quite right they'd undoubtedly re-shoot it.

DJ: As far as exaggerating the rotoscope, was that easy for you?

GN: I can't remember any problems and, of course, we had the moviolas.

We could run it over and over again. As I said, in that one scene we threw out one hundred [rotoscoped] drawings. We didn't use it.

DJ: Because there's still a stretch and squash, even in Snow White, but it's different than the dwarfs.

GN: Oh yes. We wouldn't dare all of a sudden overdo it or something. You had to be very cautious, but we tried to get it into the drawing. See, we re-drew the rotoscope. Her chin was down to her bosom. She was about five heads high, or something, but the girl was probably seven heads high, so we picked it up by making a trim little [figure]. We moved the waistline up and moved the neckline down and tried to overcome difficulties by making a brace-less outer collar. We changed her enough and we trimmed her down, of course. If her skirt was out too long, too far, [we'd] perform a little arc and twist it the other way. We did everything that we would like to see happen.

DJ: Who's we?

GN: Marc [Davis] and even Les Novros. And I primarily made the changes. But after we did it, we re-shot some of [our animation] and ran it and all looked at it at once, and if there was something I wanted to point out, I'd say "Be sure to catch this." Marc was a brilliant artist and Les was an excellent artist. Any problem that came up while they were drawing, either of them, they'd just bring it over to me and say, "Can we change this?" and if it seemed easy to do and there was no reason not to do it, we would do it. Oh, I've seen rotoscopes that didn't work at all.

DJ: For Snow White?

GN: No, not in *Snow White*, but in Fleischer they used some of it and you'd know it's been traced. You've got to overcome the fact that this is traced photography and still get this nice svelte drawing in there that made her feminine.

DJ: Did this come easy to you in the beginning or did you have to gradually get it to where you felt comfortable with it?

GN: We had to work it over and if we discovered something that worked, we'd tell each other.

DJ: When you worked on the key scenes for Snow White, did you start with the head or did you start with the body?

GN: You usually start with the head. That proportions everything else. The girl was probably close to five heads high. Very often if it was the first few heads we'd draw we would be sure they were the right height. So that was where some of the artists who work with rotoscope get off. They get the head a little too big or too small and that throws everything else off. There's no way you can overcome it, so we watched that very carefully.

DJ: Did you ever look at any of Ham Luske's scenes and think: "This could be better"?

GN: I never looked at one of his scenes, except when they appeared in the first test reel or something.

DJ: And what did you think, then?

GN: I never thought of it as being Ham's, really. He was one of the fellows that I respected very highly and I don't think I ever talked the character over with him at any time. I can't recall it. I'm sure he looked at some of my scenes in the finished picture and realized that they worked and I did the same with his. [Marc Davis went into detail on how Grim thought Hams' early efforts on the heroine "looked like shit."]

DJ: Did Jack Campbell ever discuss with you any of the problems he might be having with Snow White?

GN: Never, never once. But Jack had been a professional artist before he ever got into animation, so he was one of the good.... Walt had a bunch of wonderful [draughtsmen]. Without great draughtsmen, he could not have made *Snow White*. There were good enough artists at other studios to draw the dwarfs. But in fellows like Bill Tytla and Freddie Moore and those guys, you had superb artists, superb animation artists.

DJ: Do you remember Norman Ferguson? He drew the witch.

GN: [There was] probably not a better [animation] artist in the world, Russia, Denmark, England, or anywhere else, who could have done what he did [with] it. He grew up on Broadway and he had a natural sense of exaggeration. His problem, if he had any, was going too far. And possibly he did that because he was not the greatest draughts-man, and so what he picked up [was] by going to vaudeville every week and having a high sense of the theatrical.

DJ: Do you remember looking at his drawings of the witch when you were doing Snow White?

GN: Oh yeah. Not while he was working on *Snow White*, earlier on. At one time he was a couple of [desks from me]. When I was starting in the business and hadn't been there too long, I had the desk two desks away from him, and I knew him personally, because he was one of the New Yorkers. I used to take my drawings over to him and ask him, "How does this look?" or "What do you think?" or "Have I stretched it too far?" He was a nice, quiet-spoken fellow.

DJ: But do you remember looking at his witch drawings?

GN: Oh yes, because, of course, sometimes the two characters appeared in the same scene. I thought he did a superb job. I didn't visit him while he was working on the witch, but when I first started I knew him well enough that I went deliberately into his office and said, "How many feet of animation a week do they expect here?" And he gave me a brush-off answer. He said, "I sometimes do fifteen feet a day." I remember one character we did at Walt's … a fellow came up from the front office and said, "Walt will be satisfied if we get a foot and a half a week out of this." They were caricature drawings, but they were pretty slow to work on.

DJ: You had to draw Snow White from every angle, of course?

GN: Apparently yes, but we were lucky, or else the camera move may have helped. But in three of the best art schools in the world for about eight years of going to life classes every night for that long, you learn something about drawing.

DJ: And the animation is something that you yourself had a feel for?

GN: Yeah, they always called me a natural animator. I never was aware of that, but I was told it by many of the people I worked with. Particularly, at the first studio I worked at, the Hearst Studio, I began doing things that the animators had never tried. But that was because I'd been drawing in life classes for three quarters of a year. How many drawings would that be? Several thousands of nude bodies in all kinds of positions.

DJ: Can you recall what were your earliest scenes from *Snow White* after the easy experimental-type ones you described earlier?

GN: The first ones I think [were] where she's walking in the woods. [Actually, Grim's earliest scenes were of Snow White in the cottage, after wiping off the fireplace mantle, with the line: "It's covered with dust!"]

DJ: The sequences were not drawn in the order they appear in the film were they?

GN: No, the first scenes were not complicated ones. I think they did that on purpose. For instance, her scene with the huntsman, I think, is the best scene I had in there. I felt later, after she had gone through the forest, holding the bird on her finger, was a very touching scene. There were some scenes I wasn't satisfied with, but I didn't think they were enough to hurt the picture, and I knew that a lot of higher-ups had seen them and said OK.

Interviewed in Winter 1988.

Shamus Culhane (1908–1996)

When legendary animator Shamus Culhane passed away on February 2, 1996, journalist Lawrence Van Gelder wrote in *The New York Times*:

> Mr. Culhane was born in Ware, Mass., on November 12, 1908. When he was a small child, the family moved to Manhattan. His father, James, worked for the Interborough Rapid Transit Company. His mother, the former Alma LaPierre, was a housewife. When Mr. Culhane was 6, his father took him to a vaudeville house where the boy saw Winsor McCay, one of the earliest film cartoonists, show his animated film *Gertie the Dinosaur*.

> Mr. Culhane began drawing as a child, winning medals for his work while a student at Public School 82 in Yorkville and at Boy's High School in Harlem, then the only city high school to offer commercial art courses. After a trip to the Metropolitan Museum of Art, he decided to become an artist.

> When his father abandoned the family, the 16-year-old Mr. Culhane, the eldest of three children, quit school to support them. Walter Lantz, his best friend's brother, was then the head of animation for J.R. Bray, the first person to make theatrically distributed cartoons, and Mr. Lantz got Mr. Culhane a job as office boy.

> In 1925, covering for a drunken animator, Mr. Culhane animated his first scene—a monkey with a hot towel. In the next 62 years, working for 18 different cartoon studios, including his own, Shamus Culhane would become one of the world's foremost character animators.

> [Shamus Culhane was hired by Disney on May 29, 1935, and resigned on May 15, 1939.] He was the only animator who worked on all of the first four animated feature cartoons: Disney's *Snow White and the Seven Dwarfs* (1937) and *Pinocchio* (1940), for which Mr. Culhane animated the fox and cat selling Pinocchio to the Pleasure Island coachman; Max Fleischer's *Gulliver's Travels* (1939); and Dave Fleischer's *Mr. Bug Goes to Town* (1941), with its Hoagy Carmichael-Frank Loesser score.

Mr. Culhane also animated such characters as Krazy Kat, Betty Boop, Popeye, Pluto ('the essence of dog,' Mr. Culhane called him), and Woody Woodpecker, whose surreal personality Mr. Culhane helped develop in a series of shorts he directed for Mr. Lantz in the 1940s.

In *The 50 Greatest Cartoons as Selected by 1,000 Animation Professionals*, a book published in 1994 by Turner Broadcasting, Mr. Culhane was represented as the director of *The Barber of Seville* (1944), in which Woody shaves a construction worker while singing "Largo al factotum" from Rossini's *Barber of Seville*, matching the language's large proportion of vowels to consonants with an agility of movement possible only in animation.

In the realm of commercials, Mr. Culhane produced, directed, wrote, and often animated commercials, including the Ajax cleanser elves moving to music and the words, "Use Ajax—boom boom—the foaming cleanser;" and the classic Muriel cigar spot, with Edie Adams delivering its Mae West parody line, "Why don't you come up and smoke me some time?"

Mr. Culhane tended to view the world through an animator's eyes. As he once watched another significant world figure, Richard M. Nixon, during the Watergate scandal, he said, "Nixon always moves as if he's three frames out of sync."

As the head of the Paramount cartoon studio in 1966 and 1967, Mr. Culhane produced the Mighty Thor cartoons for television. In the late 1970s, he ran against the cost-cutting style of so-called limited animation by producing, directing, and co-writing (with a cousin, John Culhane) a series of fully animated ABC prime-time television specials: *Noah's Animals* (1976), the story of Noah from the animals' point of view, and two sequels, *King of the Beasts* and *Last of the Red-Hot Dragons*.

Mr. Culhane was the author of an autobiography, *Talking Animals and Other People*, published by St. Martin's Press in 1986, and *Animation from Script to Screen*, an explanation of animation technique published by St. Martin's in 1988.

Shamus Culhane: I was quite confident [when I heard about Walt doing a feature picture] that it'd be good.

David Johnson: I'm surprised, because no one else was.

SC: I was gung-ho about Walt. I'd been seeing his work get better and better for several years, and ours wasn't. Everybody else was [doing the] same old junk. And so I was very anxious to get in there....

One of the things about Walt: his movies are different than other pictures made at the time. He would pile in things that you'd never see if you saw the picture *once*. But if you saw it two, three, four times, you kept finding things.

I worked on [*Snow White* for] about four months. I think I got just about the last piece of animation, except for the old prince and the jittery horse.

[Regarding Dopey's "out-of-stepness"]

I got my version of it from a Laurel and Hardy feature movie, *Laurel and Hardy in India* [*Bonnie Scotland*]. They had this marvelous sequence where Hardy was like a top sergeant or something, so he was walking outside of the group. I don't know how they did it or who they used, but literally they had thousands of people in a long shot all marching in uniform with rifles and packs and stuff, winding down a mountainside, way out of sight. It seems Hardy thought Laurel was out of step, so he made him get in step, and he hopped, and he skipped, and he jumped. And when he did, he made everybody else hop and skip all the way down there, as far as you could see.

DJ: So that was your idea?

SC: It wasn't my idea. But they showed me how to do it.

DJ: Did Ben Sharpsteen tell you he got it from the movie?

SC: No, I saw the movie. They gave it to me to learn how to do it.

DJ: That's never mentioned. What you just told me is new to me.

SC: Yeah, I'd forgotten all about it.

[Moving to another subject.]

A whole group of us had a whole day a week of art classes and usually the morning might be in the zoo. The live model was always in the afternoon. Now in the morning we might [also] have a piece of drapery to draw. Drapery is a bitch to draw. I mean, we're not used to drapery. We don't wear anything that drapes. So it's very difficult for you to understand the difference in the fold of wool or silk. This place was like no other, remotely. It fulfilled my wildest dreams.

Interviewed in September 1987.

Ollie Johnston
(1912–2008)

Warmth was undoubtedly the main trademark of Ollie Johnston's animation. Whereas Milt Kahl was known for his tremendous draftsmanship, Woolie Reitherman for his action scenes, and Frank Thomas for his analytical skills, Ollie, the last of the Nine Old Men, will undoubtedly be remembered by future generations for having instilled in all his characters the most Disney of all qualities: "heart."

Born in Palo Alto, California, on October 31, 1912, Ollie attended grammar school on the campus of Stanford University, where his father served as professor of Romance languages. After graduating from Palo Alto High School, he returned to Stanford and spent his last year of study at Chouinard Art Institute in Los Angeles.

On January 21, 1935, Ollie joined Disney as an inbetweener, tackling shorts that included *Mickey's Garden* (1935) and *Mickey's Rival* (1936). On March 23, 1936, he became Freddy Moore's assistant, working on Silly Symphonies, including *The Tortoise and the Hare* (1935), *More Kittens* (1936), and *Little Hiawatta* (1937), as well as a few Mickey shorts like *Mickey's Garden* (1935). Ollie also assisted Freddy on the animation of the dwarfs in *Snow White and the Seven Dwafs*. Ollie became a full-fledged animator on *The Brave Little Tailor* (1938), in which he animated the townspeople. Other shorts that he tackled throughout the years include *The Pointer* (1939), *The Practical Pig* (1940), *Mickey's Surprise Party* (1939), *How to Play Baseball* (1940), *Chicken Little* (1943), *Reason and Emotion* (1943), *The Pelican and the Snipe* (1944), *Susie, the Little Blue Coupe* (1951), and *Ben and Me* (1953).

Ollie's contribution to 24 animated features is nothing short of staggering. He handled Pinocchio talking to the Blue Fairy in *Pinocchio*; the centaurettes and cupids in "The Pastoral Symphony" sequence of *Fantasia*; Baby Bambi and Thumper in *Bambi*; The Flying Gauchito in *The Three Caballeros*; Casey at the Bat and Peter and the

Wolf in *Make Mine Music*, Br'er Rabbit in *Song of the South*, Little Toot and Johnny Appleseed in *Melody Time*; most of the characters in *The Adventures of Ichabod and Mr. Toad*; the stepsisters and the lackey in *Cinderella*; Alice and the King of Hearts in *Alice in Wonderland*; Mr. Smee in *Peter Pan*; Lady, Jock, and Trusty in *Lady and the Tramp*; the good fairies in *Sleeping Beauty*; Pongo, Perdita, Nanny Cook, and the puppies in *101 Dalmatians*; Merlin, Wart, and Archimedes in *The Sword in the Stone*; the penguins as waiters in *Mary Poppins*; Baloo, Bagheera, Mowgli, and the Girl in *The Jungle Book*; Amelia, Abigail, and Uncle Waldo in *The Aristocats*; Prince John, Sir Hiss, Robin Hood, Little John, and Maid Marian in *Robin Hood*; Penny, Orville, Bernard, Bianca, and Rufus in *The Rescuers*; Pooh and Piglet in *The Many Adventures of Winnie the Pooh*; and finally young Todd, young Copper, Chief, Vixey, and Tod in *The Fox and the Hound*.

An avid train enthusiast, in his spare time Ollie created a back-yard railroad at his home and was instrumental in helping stir Walt Disney's own personal interest in trains.

After 43 years with the studio, Ollie retired in 1978. He went on to co-author four books with his long-time friend Frank Thomas, beginning with the definitive *Disney Animation: The Illusion of Life*, followed by *Too Funny For Words, Walt Disney's Bambi: The Story and the Film*, and *The Disney Villain*. He and Frank were also the subjects of the 1995 documentary *Frank and Ollie*, directed by Frank's son Ted Thomas which chronicles their unique friendship which began at Stanford, and creative relationship at Disney.

That same year, Disney artists also paid tribute to the legendary elder animators in the Mickey Mouse featurette *Runaway Brain* by creating a villain whimsically named "Dr. Frankenollie." Frank and Ollie later made cameo appearances in two Brad Bird movies: *The Iron Giant* and *The Incredibles*.

Ollie Johnston died April 14, 2008.

[About Freddie Moore.]

Ollie Johnston: [His home] was not too far from the studio. He had me and Frank Thomas and Larry Clemmons and Scott Whitaker and Bill Grey, and everybody that was associated with him over to his place one night. I can't remember if it was the one house he built or earlier.

David Johnson: What was he like as a person?

OJ: In what way?

DJ: I know he was kind of uncomplicated.

OJ: He was very definite but not eloquent in what he wanted. He would tell me or Frank who preceded me there what he wanted very definitely, whether it was half drawing and half talking. He wasn't eloquent in a lot of ways, but Walt always brought all the visitors in to see Fred, because Fred drew rapidly and with such a beautiful line. Walt always wanted Fred to draw over Tytla's stuff.

DJ: Oh, he did?

OJ: Oh yeah. Because it was not as appealing.

DJ: I know you came in 1935, but you must have come in the early part of 1935.

OJ: January. Frank came in September. Thor Putnam came first. He preceded Frank by a couple of weeks. Frank decided he ought to wait at least that long, because they might not be taking people that fast. And so he came later that month. Actually I wanted to continue my studies with Pruett Carter at Chouinard Art Institute and go back to New York and pick out an illustrator [job], because I loved getting the emotions into the drawings. Frank and I were living together by then, in a boarding house. I had transferred from Stanford. I went there about three years plus, and came down here and saw what Frank was doing, because he had graduated. At Stanford we had about two classes where you did landscape chalk drawings, there were perspective drawings, there were history of art. I had taken all of those courses and was driving up to San Mateo. You could pay five bucks to get in and draw a model, no teacher. But anyway I came down with the football team (I was the manager) and visited Frank. Frank showed me the stuff he was doing and I said, "If I don't get elected senior manager I'm going to come down here in January." And fortunately I didn't get elected. Another guy did. There was a lot of politics in that.

DJ: You didn't graduate then?

OJ: They were giving me credit at Chouinard. The dean at Stanford, Dean Corbourn said, "We'll work it out so you get credit there and you can come back and graduate when you're ready." So that's what I decided to do. My dad was a professor there. Head of the department of Romantic Languages. My dad agreed and somehow scraped up money to pay my tuition. You know, professors weren't paid much in those days, even though he was head of the department.

DJ: This was the Depression.

OJ: So I came down and started in. Don Graham was a Stanford man. He was a good artist, but very studied. In other words, you wouldn't find him doing an emotional scene with animation. Anyway, that morning I woke up, and Frank was getting ready to go out to the studio. This was in January, I think. And he said, "They want you to come and take a tryout." Apparently Don Graham had told them that I should be out there at the studio. They were looking for people. So, geese, my dad just paid this tuition, what am I going to do? I worked out some deal where I could get a lot of paper and pens and pencils and stuff instead of being there to do the artwork. So I decided I'll take a tryout and stay there for a year or so and make some money and pay my dad back. Because I was concerned about him and my mother. But I just fell in love with it. You have emotional stuff in paintings, but this is really great because I can bring it to life. So that's what I did.

DJ: How long were you with George Drake in the inbetween department?

OJ: That's hard to say, because they began assigning the stuff to other animators, the clean-ups. Like to Geronimi.

DJ: How many weeks in training?

OJ: You had to do some tests. I must have been there three months.

DJ: And that was under George Drake, too?

OJ: Terrible man. Yeah, I did stuff for other guys, and finally I got assigned to do something for Geronimi in *Mickey's Rival* where he has the bull in the car. I told Frank, "You know I'm going to do this so damn good and make Geronimi's stuff look so damn good that somebody's going to notice it and do something for me." So I did.

DJ: Had you met Walt by this time?

OJ: Yeah, but you didn't get intimate with him.

DJ: Were you at the annex when you were doing this or were you in the main building?

OJ: I think it was the main building. I was in the annex for a couple of weeks or something. Anyhow, I cleaned up this stuff and I got a call one day from Jaxon [Wilfred Jackson] and he said, "Come up to the sweatbox." So I went up, figuring I'm going to be fired, [that I had] ruined the scene. I walked in and he said, "These are the best goddamn cleanups I ever saw!" So Geronimi immediately wanted me to work for him, but I stalled, because I didn't like his work particularly. And at that point Fred lost his assistant, a guy named Smith who went into animation, and he tried Thor Putnam and that didn't work out, and he tried somebody else who didn't work out. And Frank said, "Why don't you try Ollie?" So he tried me and we clicked.

DJ: How long did you work with him?

OJ: From March 26, 1936, to 1937 when we finished work [on *Snow White*].

DJ: So you were doing other things for a whole year before you got to Fred Moore?

OJ: Yeah, I guess so. We had to do personal tests. I didn't keep track of that. I just knew I was better than a lot of the guys. I had a feeling for animation, I've always had. All the guys in Fred's crew, none of them turned out to be animators.

DJ: So when you started in March, 1936, he was already starting to do the dwarfs, then?

OJ: No, he just was waiting to get his first scene. He didn't even have a scene. His first scene was with Dopey with the soap. It was later re-drawn by Fred Spencer.

DJ: Would there be a reason why Fred would have done these [dwarf model sheets] in February and then not get a scene until another month?

OL: Yeah, they didn't have the story stuff ready.

DJ: So you were with him when he got his first scene with the soap, then?

OJ: I moved in a little before that. I tried to remember the date, because I said, "This is going to change my life." March 26, 1936.

DJ: Do you remember being in story meetings about Deafy?

OJ: I was called in to a meeting along with Frank and some other guys. I wasn't an animator yet. I don't know why I was called in to the meeting. We sat up on some bleachers there on the soundstage. And Walt talked to us about the picture. He went through and described the whole thing, and some of the guys got up and tried to imitate how the characters would walk and various things. They had probably had another meeting like that before I ever got there.

DJ: And Deafy was discussed at that time?

OJ: I think he was gone by the time I moved in with Fred. [Looking at Doc drawings with the lens by Fred.] Fred had this great way letting everything drag.

DJ: Would you say Fred was a very fun-loving person, or did he get moody?

OJ: He'd get into these states of mind where he couldn't get started with a scene. Wasn't so much [that] he was moody, [he would] just wander around, [and] couldn't get going. So he'd say, "Hey, tell me how good I am!" So we'd all start saying, "Hey, Fred, you're the greatest. Michelangelo couldn't even work with you, you're so good." Pretty soon he'd say, "Wait a minute, stop, I'm not that good!" and then he'd start drawing.

DJ: Who were his favorite artists? Did he ever mention anything like that?

OJ: I don't really remember him having any stuff pinned up around the room that was fine art.

DJ: Did he ever mention anything about Rembrandt or Raphael or Leonardo or any of those that he particularly admired?

OJ: He'd be more likely to mention Paddyhook (?) or one of those guys who drew cheesecake drawings or the guys drawing for *The New Yorker*.

DJ: Illustrators?

OJ: Yeah, because they came in and were introduced to him when they would come to the studio. When Fairbanks and Pickford came, why they were always in Fred's room. So I always got to see those people. The door's over here, I'm here, and Fred's over here.

DJ: This was on the first (ground) floor?

OJ: That's right. Inside is the parking lot. ... And Russell Paterson, a famous cartoonist was in to see him. Lot of those people. I kind of have the feeling that they were more his idols. Though Fred was pretty damn good. He drew the keenest women. I had a lot of those. Andreas [Deja] has those now.

DJ: Would the soundtrack be on 78 disc or on film?

OJ: On film.

DJ: Even on *Snow White*?

OJ: Yes. One of the funniest things was running it backwards.

DJ: I was told the pilot scene was the one around the bed.

OJ: Yes, Fred did that.

DJ: Where you present when they actually showed that?

OJ: Oh yeah, I did some work on it.

Interviewed on February 20, 2001.

Art Babbitt
(1907–1992)

The man who led the strike and the man who "created" Goofy: in a way, those two images of Art Babbitt do summarize a man who was both a marvelous artist and a very controversial personality.

Babbitt started animating in 1924 and by 1929 had joined the Paul Terry Studio. In 1932, after having seen *The Skeleton Dance*, he decided to apply at Disney and managed to enter the studio in July 1932. His first projects as a Disney animator included various Silly Symphonies and Mickey shorts. Among them: *The Klondike Kid* (1932), *Santa's Workshop* (1932), *The Mad Doctor* (1933), *Ye Olden Days* (1933), *Mickey's Gala Premiere* (1933), *Lullaby Land* (1933), *The Steeple Chase* (1933), *The Pet Store* (1933), *The China Shop* (1933), *The Grasshopper and the Ants* (1934), *Playful Pluto* (1934), *Gulliver Mickey* (1934), *Funny Little Bunnies* (1934), *Peculiar Penguins* (1934), *The Goddess of Spring* (1934), *Two-Gun Mickey* (1934), *Water Babies* (1935), *Mickey's Garden* (1935), *Broken Toys* (1935), *Mickey's Polo Team* (1935), *Polar Trappers* (1938), and *Ferdinand the Bull* (1938).

Amazingly, during those formative years at Disney, Babbitt already tackled some of his greatest "roles": the Big Bad Wolf and some of the pigs' scenes in *The Three Little Pigs* (1933), the mayor in *The Pied Piper* (1933), Abner Mouse in *The Country Cousin* (1936) and Donald Duck that he animated in his first screen appearance, *The Wise Little Hen* (1934), along with Dick Huemer.

In *Mickey's Service Station* (1935), Babbitt handled Goofy for the first time and instantly started developing his on-screen personality, adding to it little by little in the shorts that followed: *On Ice* (1935), *Moving Day* (1936), *Moose Hunters* (1937), *Mickey's Amateurs* (1937), *Lonesome Ghosts* (1937), *The Whalers* (1938), *Goofy and Wilbur* (1939), *Goofy's Glider* (1940), *Baggage Buster* (1941), and *The Art of Self Defense* (1941).

In 1932 Babbitt was also instrumental in the establishment of the studio night classes that would soon be taught by Don Graham.

Before leading the 1941 strike of the Disney Studio, Art Babbitt moved to the animated features, starting with *Snow White* on which he animated much of the Queen and several scenes of the Dwarfs, most notably Doc's "debut" scene with the diamond selection and Dopey's wary walk upstairs to the bedroom. On *Pinocchio*, Babbitt was in charge of Geppetto, which he considered his best animation ever. On *Fantasia* he focused on the mushroom Chinese dance and on the Russian ballet from the "Nutcracker" sequence while also tackling Zeus and Vulcan in the "Pastoral Symphony." Finally, he animated the stork in *Dumbo*.

After the strike, Art Babbitt was hired back briefly by the studio. From 1943 to 1947 (when he left Disney for good), Babbitt animated on five shorts: *The Flying Jalopy* (1943), *How to Play Football* (1944), *Bootle Beetle* (1947), *Foul Hunting* (1947), *They're Off* (1948), and on the "Bongo" sequence in *Fun and Fancy Free* (1947).

In 1949, Art Babbitt joined UPA that had been created a few years earlier by former Disney artists that had been involved in the strike: Dave Hilberman, Zachary Schwartz, and Steve Bosustow. At UPA, Babbitt animated the first Jolly Frolics cartoon, *Ragtime Bear* (1949), which introduced Mr. Magoo. One of his greatest UPA achievements was the last of the Jolly Frolics shorts, John Hubley's *Rooty Toot Toot*, on which he handled the animation along with Grim Natwick.

Babbitt's association with Hubley carried on even after Art left UPA in 1952. Between 1966 and 1975 Babbitt headed Hanna-Barbera's commercial department and worked on some of the projects that Hubley directed, like the short *Of Men and Demons* (1969) and the TV special "Everybody Rides the Carousel" (1975).

In the mid-70s, in addition to teaching classes at Richard Williams' animation studio in London, Babbitt, along with Grim Natwick, animated sequences from *Raggedy Ann and Andy* (1978) and *The Thief and the Cobbler*.

Art Babbitt died March 4, 1992.

[Talking about the origin of the Disney art school and when the classes were originally held at his home in Hollywood]

Art Babbitt: It did cause trouble when they let girls get into the class, because they'd make wisecracks about the models. So I had to lay down the law. I said, "If I hear anybody making a wisecrack about the models, out you go!"

[On composer Frank Churchill]

I would practice [piano] on the soundstage during lunch time [Note: Art was taking piano lessons at the time], and I was struggling with this particular [Chopin] étude, and Churchill came in and said, "Gee, that sounds familiar," and sat down and played it beautifully. Frank would come into the studio on Friday, for example, with a bag full of gin bottles and on Monday morning all the gin bottles would be gone, and five or six songs would come out. We went on a Grace Line cruise—a group from Disney: Les Clark, Dick Lundy, so on— and Frank was plastered all the time. Frank and Les and I shared a stateroom and [once] Frank was so drunk there was absolutely no movement in his body at all. I called the doctor to see if the guy was dead or not. Frank was always trying to commit suicide. We spent seventeen days together on that ship and it was all I could do to keep him from jumping overboard. There was this constant battle. I assume it had something to do with the death of his first wife. But he had a daughter in a private Catholic school somewhere up in Flintridge [La Cañada, California] and this daughter was the light of his life. He kept a picture by his bedside which was not the picture of [his second wife] Carolyn Shaefer—it was the picture of another woman—evidently his first wife. [Note: According to Carolyn's close friend Teresa Smith, Frank was never sure if the daughter was actually Frank's.] You couldn't get him to talk about [his musical background]. He didn't reveal anything. [He was] very contained. This was a man who was set to destroy himself.

[On Wilfred Jackson]

[He was] the best director they had. He was a bright man, a no-nonsense man. He knew what he was doing. He didn't try to impress you. He was an honest man, a competent man.

[On Dave Hand]

[I would tell him,] "Come on Dave, stop trying to be a boy scout. [Dave,] "And what's wrong with the Boy Scouts?"

[On Ben Sharpsteen]

"See, I told you it could be done in four feet," [said Ben]. "No Ben, that was *twelve* feet!"

[On being assigned to the queen in *Snow White*]

I remember being taken off the Goofy stuff that I'd been working on and being put on *Snow White*. But it's like in an automobile factory: you're no longer putting on hubcaps. From now on you're doing steering wheels. It's an assignment, so I'll do it. But here I go from Goofy to the queen. It's a hell of a big jump. [Note: Actually Babbitt went from drawing Dopey and other dwarfs, of which he did several scenes, to the queen.]

[On drawing the queen]

I was very insecure about it. Very insecure. When I did a test that turned out well, I was the most delighted and surprised person in the world. Because I always felt, innately, "Jesus, this is going to be lousy." And there were times, like on *Country Cousin*, when I couldn't wait for vacation time to come around, because I hated the goddam thing. I couldn't bear to work on it anymore, and this is the one that won the Oscar in 1936.

The voice, the characterization that's in the voice has a lot to do with [the Queen's] behavior.

[On getting off on the voice synchronization]

There's no excuse for it! Because if you have an accurate reading, there are only two places where your lip sync can be correct. One is right on, and the other one—if you're desperate and working on twos—one frame before. Never anyplace else. Never a frame late, never!

Interviewed in September 1987.

George Rowley (1905–1991)

Effects animator George Rowley was born on June 23, 1905, in Iowa. He studied at the Art Institute in Chicago and was hired by Disney as an inbetweener in 1934. He was one of the first artists animating in the newly formed effects department spearheaded by Cy Young in early 1935. While at the studio he tackled many shorts and most of the features, from *Snow White and the Seven Dwarfs* to *Lady and the Tramp*. He was laid off on December 17, 1954. After leaving Disney he worked for several other animation studios, including Famous Studios and Hanna-Barbera.

George Rowley retired in the 1970s and died August 18, 1991.

David Johnson: When did you begin at the studio and how?

George Rowley: I began at the studio in 1934 and I went over and applied for a job and I became an inbetweener.

DJ: Was it $15 a week like everybody else?

GR: Yeah.

DJ: What was your background?

GR: I had studied at [the] Art Institute in Chicago [in the 1920s]. And I also studied at the Art Academy in Chicago. And I went to the art school in Omaha, Nebraska.

DJ: Was it your ambition to be a fine artist or commercial artist?

GR: Commercial artist. I did commercial art. All sorts of things like Christmas cards and what have you, to get along. Actually, the real reason I came out to California was because my father became ill and we had to change climate. That's the reason. So I went to Disney to get a job there in 1934. I worked there until 1955.

DJ: How did you find out that they were hiring?

GR: I didn't find out. I just went there and applied!

DJ: Did you apply at many other studios, too?

GR: Not really, no.

DJ: Was that your first job in California?

GR: That was my first job. I had other jobs, but they were not art jobs.

DJ: How long had you been in California before that?

GR: I came to California in 1930. That was right in the middle of the Depression.

DJ: So you were doing other things during those four years.

GR: Yes, I've done everything. In fact, I look back and I wonder how I survived, really. [Laughs] But, you know, those things come and go.

DJ: What were some of the other things that you did?

GR: I did some sign painting, I did some Christmas cards. I washed some windows. I'd do all kinds of things. I maintained an apartment by doing janitorial work there and that sort of thing.

DJ: And what happened that gave you the impetus, after four years of doing all of this stuff, to go to the Disney Studio?

GR: Right at that time the *Three Little Pigs* came out, and I was impressed by that. I said, "That'll be fun to do."

DJ: So when you came you were put as an inbetweener. Was George Drake there at the time?

GR: Yes.

DJ: I've heard all about him.

GR: I dare say you didn't hear anything good about him.

DJ: No, I didn't. The poor man was quite crazy, I understand.

GR: He was insane.

DJ: Did Ken Anderson come about the same time that you did?

GR: Just about the same time, yeah.

DJ: Who were some of the others that came [at that time]?

GR: Jim Algar, Ed Aardal, Tony Rivera, Campbell Grant....

DJ: So you were at the studio at the very beginning of _Snow White_?

GR: Oh yes, I was there before _Snow White_ was started.

DJ: What was your reaction when you found out about _Snow White_?

GR: You knew what they're working on. You knew they were working on a feature-length picture. It isn't somebody comes along and says, "Hey, George, we're going to do a feature-length picture."

DJ: You weren't given a memo or anything from Walt that said so.

GR: No, no, no. Of course we did receive memos from Walt all the time, not necessarily pertaining to _Snow White_. But, "If you think of a gag, you turn it in." Maybe get $10 for it or something. And then, of course, when they did eventually start to think seriously about _Snow White_, then they had definite meetings about _Snow White_, of naming the dwarfs, giving their descriptions, their personalities, and that sort of thing.

DJ: Were you there at the beginning of those meetings?

GR: Yes.

DJ: Can you recall anything about those early meetings?

GR: All I remember is that the storymen   would get up and give you a definition of each dwarf, or any character. For instance, Dopey, they'd call him a flannel-mouth person, that sort of thing.

DJ: Ken Anderson said that [Walt] acted out every part.

GR: That's right, he did. He acted out every part. He was a very unusual person. I never knew anybody like him. I have worked for some of the other directors like Cecil B. DeMille, for instance. I never met anybody like him.

We would do other pictures preparatory to _Snow White_. For instance, _Goddess of Spring_.

DJ: Were you still in animation at that time or had you gone into special effects?

GR: During that process I went into special effects sometime after that. I was very happy to do it and to get away from George Drake. That guy made me nuts.

DJ: Did Cy Young come to the studio after you did?

GE: No, he was there before me.

DJ: And then you guys, Ugo D'Orsi, Cy Young, and you and a couple of others...

GR: Josh Meador.

DJ: ...had a regular special effects department. Now that was right around the time of *Snow White*. That was the catalyst, wasn't it?

GR: Yeah.

DJ: Can you talk about this, about the building of the special effects department?

GR: When the animators were doing character work, they would say, "Why do I have to do all this water? Why do I have to do all these branches? Why do I have to do fire? Why do I have to this, that, and the other thing?" Walt said, "We'll have a special effects department." He asked Cy Young to start it. He was the impetus of it. Cy did start it and, of course, he had to have some helpers. By that time I was probably a clean-up-man, or an assistant as the case may be. So then they chose myself and Josh Meador and Cornet Wood and Stan Quackenbush. About that many. There were others, but their names escape me.

So then whenever the animators would have something like, for instance, Snow White running through the woods after the huntsman had tried to stab her ... I did all those trees and that's just an example. When she's singing in the well, I think Stan Quackenbush did the pigeons, and the water in the well and that sort of thing. We became the effects department. Then it evolved so that when we have sweatboxes for the pencil animation, there would be a rough, without effects. Eventually Josh Meador and I became the ones who would go up and say what the effects would be. So then we evolved into being not only effects animators but supervisors. We would have ten or twelve animators working under us and we would supervise that animation.

DJ: You would be in the sweat box sitting there seeing every scene....

GR: And stipulate what kind of shadows, for instance ... the branches grabbing Snow White or the changes of the queen into the witch and all that sort of thing. Sometimes the effects and the character were so closely related that you had to do both.

DJ: Can you recall any particular instance?

GR: I can't in *Snow White*. But in *Fantasia*, for instance, when Mickey Mouse as the sorcerer's apprentice is involved in all that water. There were times when....

DJ: Ugo d'Orsi did that.

GR: Not all of it.

DJ: Oh, you did some of it?

GR: Oh, of course. He didn't do all of it. He did *some* of it. He's a very capable man.

DJ: Tell me a little bit about Cy Young. What was your impression of Cy Young? What do you remember?

GR: He was just a person I worked with. He was not difficult to get along with and he was an amiable guy. I didn't dislike him in any way. In fact, I sort of liked the guy.

DJ: He was quiet, I understand.

GR: Very quiet.

DJ: And always spoke with an accent.

GR: I don't remember what happened to him. He just left, I guess. So when he left, then I became supervisor of the effects department along, again, with Josh Meador. We both took directors with us.

GR: Wasn't there Jack Boyd?

GR: No, Jack Boyd didn't come till later.

DJ: Ugo d'Orsi was the real impetuous one, and worked a lot with Cy Young. Once, they were studying the way the flames would be on this cauldron. I suppose it was from *Snow White*.

GR: He wasn't the only one. I was there, too.

DJ: They had this terrible argument because one said, "No, it should be black only where the flames are there," and the other one said, "Oh no, it should be black all around there." They had this argument and they had this fire going on at the time. The smoke was coming all over the place. So finally they had to put the fire out because everyone was walking down the hall and the smoke was getting under the doors.

GR: That's a little exaggerated, I think. Extremely exaggerated.

DJ: You were there.

GR: I was there.

DJ: Could you describe it from your point of view?

GR: Ugo d'Orsi was very temperamental. He was an Italian and he would rage on. But [he was] not a mean guy at all. He was just temperamental. Cy was an Oriental and he was *very calm*. They sometimes disagreed. In this particular instance, d'Orsi, like anybody who does animation, puts some of himself in that. Just like anybody. You can't just animate a waterfall and do that. You always put something of yourself in there. So he did whatever he felt was right. And naturally it turned out right, whether it was fire or water, or whatever.

DJ: But they actually were building this fire there in the room?

GR: Oh yes, but that's not unusual.

DJ: That's not unusual?

GR: It was exaggerated to say that the hall was covered with smoke. That was exaggerated.

DJ: Early on did the men have their own room?

GR: Yes, everybody had their own room.

DJ: No, I mean all the special effects together in the same room?

GR: Oh, no. They all had their own rooms.

DJ: One of your duties was to assign special effects for different parts of the movie.

GR: That's right. In other words, I would go up to the sweatbox with the director and other animators, and we would determine that this scene would have such and such an effect: of pigeons and water, or the bucket that came out of the well, or whatever. And the effects department would be there. So we'd go through the whole sequence. And the secretary would write all this stuff up and send it to me and I would have a copy of it and then, when the scenes would be ready to be handed out, I'd go over it with the director, along sometimes with the animator, sometimes without. We would determine what it would be. Sometimes they wanted to elaborate on it and sometimes they didn't, in the effects. When they want to point something out, they'll elaborate on it. You have to know these things, so when you give it to one of your animators, he isn't going to try and steal the action away from the character by putting in a lot of trick effects in there. You had to watch him. Then sometimes we want the effects to be elaborate. You had to watch those.

DJ: Can you recall any particular sweatbox session where a big change in special effects was required?

GR: Not in *Snow White*.

Now these pigeons were done by the effects department. And also these ripples were done in shellac, transparent shellac. And the figure was put under the cel that had the shellac on it and over the shellac and the background was the distortion glass.

DJ: But how did they get this out of focus and yet she's basically in focus?

GR: I just told you. This is shellac.

DJ: But normally shellac is a very hard line.

GR: On a cel it is not a hard line, it just looks like it's out of focus. So we animated this in shellac, these ripples. She is under a distortion glass and so is the background.

DJ: And how many levels would this be? In other words, would this be all on one multiplane level?

GR: First comes the ripples. The ripples are above the distortion glass. They're shellac, they're transparent. They look like they're out of focus because that's how it reacts on a piece of cel. And of course, all this stuff is an overlay, this black stuff [the inside of the well]. That's the first thing, the top cel, the overlay. And then come the ripples which are done in shellac. Look like they're out of focus and they're transparent. They just naturally make things wiggly-waggly when they go by because they're shellac. Then comes the distortion glass after that. Then comes the animation of Snow White and then comes the background.

DJ: Now something like this, for instance, the shadow effects on the drapery, would that be your job?

GR: Yes.

DJ: How would you decide on how much or how little you would use?

GR: We have a layout man tell us how much he wants. It could have been [Hugh] Hennesy. It could have been [Charles] Philippi.

When using masks they make a mask for each frame: a cel with black paint on it. That is a certain amount of exposure. It usually has either 40% or 60% exposure.

DJ: And that's put over the cel.

GR: When they shoot it, they shoot it first with 40% light and then they shoot it over again with 60% light. Then if they want to dissolve it, they dissolve the mask right off of the figure, ordinarily [in] sixteen frames, sometimes twelve. The light on the camera just dissolves it off.

Ralph Hulett animated the glow around the candles. The glow around the candle is airbrush, but the reflected flicker on the wall is an animated mask which changes with each exposure. You'd shoot the whole thing with the mask, at 40%. The whole scene, everything. Then you take the mask off and you shoot the whole scene at 60%. It sounds complicated, but it's not complicated, really. It takes a lot of time, but that's what we're there for.

DJ: [In the transformation scene,] the room begins to revolve around her. Now was that animated?

GR: That was animated.

DJ: You actually had to animate the stones?

GR: That's right, yes. The background per se would move to the right. We just move the background to the right. Some of these things, like this thing, would turn, like a turntable. You'd animate that. And maybe a piece of furniture would come through here like this.

DJ: So all of the stuff that's moving is animated, but at the same time they would move to the right, pull it. Of course this was all out of focus. Was this through a diffusion?

GR: I don't remember it being that out of focus, but it would probably be out of focus with the camera, because it would be a better effect if even the moving things were out of focus than have her be out of focus. Probably the whole thing is a little out of focus.

DJ: How many cel levels [were there] for the queen with the glass?

GR: That's a held cel. Then they have a cel for the front part of the glass, just the front part. [It] has this airbrush stuff. Then they have the queen, who animates and she's looking in the glass. They have her action which registers to the glass. The glass has a thickness, by the way. This isn't a regular glass. And then they have the background. Before you have the queen, first they have the top half of glass, goes up to here. Then they have bubbles going up. Then they have the queen who is animated and the bubbles are animated as well. Then they have the back of the glass. I don't remember if the potion moved or not. But if it did [it did] the bubbles were over the queen. The color of the potion was back of the queen. And then behind that was the other part of the glass which was on a cel. It wasn't on a background because it had to match this. So that would be one cel for the glass, one cel for the held cel, one cel for the glass, one for the queen, one for the bubbles, and one cel for the potion, and then the back of the glass which would be on a cel. That's six, which is as high as you can go.

DJ: Was the steam coming out of the witch's cauldron double-exposed?

GR: Yes. ... That's a flicker cel. [Snow White in front of the fireplace.] That's probably three cels that cover this thing. And they're slightly different. You keep taking one off and putting another one on. They flicker like a fire flickers.

DJ: Who thought of that?

GR: I don't know who thought of it. Maybe I thought of it.

DJ: And the glint on the huntsman's blade, out of focus: they do a white cross on a cel and then photograph that out of focus on top of the other one?

GR: That's right.

DJ: That would be a double exposure.

GR: That's right. I think I thought of that in a sweatbox....

The paint on the back side of a cel always has sheen to it. Sometimes you want something to look dull so you would paint it on top of the cel. You wanted that boat to look dull. It's not unusual to paint on the top of the cel, because you want a certain effect. And always a cel has a certain sheen to it. But if you paint on top if it then it has a dull [effect].

DJ: These bubbles.... This is white paint?

GR: That's white paint. There're two cels with this bubble. There's the back of the bubble, which is probably a held cel. I'm not sure. There's the back of the cel, there's the front of the cel, and inbetween them is the fly.

DJ: Is this all airbrush, this white stuff?

GR: It probably is.

DJ: Or could that be slightly out-of-focus, double exposed, like with the lightning.

GR: Yeah, it could be out-of-focus, yeah.

DJ: And you think Josh Meador did that?

GR: I think he did; I'm not sure. I'm reasonably sure he did that. I can't swear to it. These things here are all out-of-focus anyway.

DJ: What about Doc's glasses. Wasn't that done with opaque paint?

GR: That's right.

DJ: The red on the witch's nose, was this done the same way as the blush on Snow White's cheek?

GR: Yeah.

DJ: Now they talk a lot about the rain in *Snow White*.

GR: The rain's animated. Every bit of it is animated. [With a cycle of stock rain, also animated.]

DJ: I read that sometimes they used real rain superimposed over it.

GR: I've never seen or heard of it. It's hard to get real rain. I mean you have to get something black. And the minute you put light on it....

DJ: Did you have fun working on *Snow White*?

GR: It was a lot of fun, because it was a new thing and it was exciting.

DJ: Is there anything that you personally thought of, regarding special effects?

GR: When she pulls the apple out of the cauldron, and the apple turns into a skull: I animated that.

Interviewed in 1988.

Libbie Meador
(1914–2008)

Elizabeth Meador was the wife of Disney effects animator Josh Meador.

Libbie Meador: I remember that we sat there in *awe* at the conclusion of the picture [*Snow White*], that there was this vast silence. My husband murmured, "I don't know how we did it." Two or three people heard and gave a little murmur of laughter, and then suddenly the applause came throughout: it was jubilant! It was such an amazing experience that it was awesome ... to think that that thing had gotten together! All those people ... those few people had done such a beautiful production.

David Johnson: Really, one of the great works of our time.

LM: It was certainly impressive to the people who worked on it.

DJ: And to everyone else. Were you in on the work that your husband was doing during the progress of this?

LM: Josh made me be a part of the whole [thing]. He wanted me to know what he was doing. He didn't isolate me from the studio ... like many wives didn't know what their husbands were doing.

DJ: You said he worked on something ... the shadows, maybe?

LM: The shadows definitely. One of the first times that transparent shadows had been used.

DJ: They did it through double exposure. That was one of the first times that it had been used: on *Snow White*. [Note: Andy Engman told me that he remembered double exposed, transparent shadows had been used when he was a young animator at Max Fleischer's.]

LN: Then the first time that animation was ever done without a line around it, Josh did in *Uncle Remus*, when he blew a square smoke ring.

He didn't put lines around it. That was a process that he developed. He was developing ideas and processes and how to do things perhaps partially from his training in physics and chemistry and so forth.

DJ: Do you remember the screening they had for *Snow White* when it was still in its rough form?

LM: Yes.

DJ: What was your reaction?

LM: I don't remember, because often when there were things like that, there was so much tension that you feel you want to get out. To see your work in progress, or their work in progress, created tremendous tension. It was created through each person's wanting to do his best work. It was not a dictate or a mandate or a feeling that Walt was criticizing you. It was that every single person there wanted to do the best work that was possible. And sometimes when they would see their work on the screen, or projected, they'd be disappointed. They wanted to do better than they were able to. So you go to a preview and it was the same thing. And people didn't discuss it very much after a show. At least the people that I knew: we didn't discuss it. Now Walt hired a movie house called the Film Art where we were shown free pictures. We were shown classical films from Europe, things that had been shot during World War I and in the twenties. These were films that he just thought that people should be exposed to as much as possible in training and learning.

What I'm trying to say is that it wasn't Walt who created the tension. Each person created his own tension. Walt was a perfectionist, that's true. He demanded the best of everybody. And he'd say, "No, do it over. No, do it over" to people. Many people resented that. They liked to do their way the first time. But some of the others who were more, let's say, gifted or talented, liked to explore what they were doing and do many different things.

DJ: You remember [that Josh] did the smoke of the magic mirror?

LM: Yes, the magic mirror and the wishing well, the water. [The bubbles for the washing-up sequence.] I am positive about that because he had me out on the deck of our apartment, out on the balcony, blowing bubbles. He'd taken a movie of it while I blew bubbles from a little pipe to get the right animation.

DJ: Wouldn't that be for *Cinderella*, because they do that in *Cinderella*.

LM: This was in *Snow White*, because *Cinderella* was later. But those first bubbles: it was definitely for *Snow White*. I know where I was living in the thirties.

And Josh definitely did the diamonds in the mines. He came home and talked with me almost every night about his work, because he knew that I was interested and because we had grown up together. I'd gone out on sketching trips with him and always we worked together.

He had a lot to do with the magic mirror and this. [I show her a photo of the queen's potion.] Yeah! That's the stuff! This is what I was looking for in these books. This pot of poison juice. This was definitely Josh's, this poison thing.

The Depression years were quite severe as far as even studying art was concerned. Most people who wanted to do it, who wanted to be artists, couldn't afford to be. And Walt advertised that he wanted artists to come to the studio to work. That's how we happened to come.

DJ: Because of the advertising?

LM: Yes. [Josh] started in 1936. We came in April 1936. Because Josh had a job in Chicago painting a mural for a department store called the Fair Store. It was 60 by 9. And that took us all that winter. We came out in the spring.

DJ: How did you like California? Because then it was beautiful, wasn't it?

LM: Yes, it was. To come from Chicago when it had been a very severe winter, and a month without sun … the whole month, 17 degrees was the highest it ever got. We drove out the Lincoln Highway through Montana, Wyoming, and into Nevada. It was all winter, all snow, snow-shoe rabbits, things that I'd never seen in the South. This expansive snow, and with farms and farms in Iowa and Nebraska, miles and miles of snow. Then to come into Nevada and down the mountain toward Reno, we saw children going to school: they had pistols strapped on their belts.

DJ: Now they carry knives to school.

LM: Real ones. And then over the mountain in Truckee and drop down the Sacramento Valley and there were peach trees in bloom.

It was awesome. Winter, almost straight down seven thousand feet, and here was spring. It was dry and brown. The climatic changes were very impressive to a person from Mississippi. Amazing. So he applied to the studio to get the job.

DJ: How long did it take for him to apply? Did he start the next day?

LM: Same week. The classes, I think, were three weeks: [he was paid] $18 a week. Then $35 a week when he went into the effects department.

DJ: You could live on that in those days.

LM: Oh, yes. $35 a week was bonanza!

DJ: Art Babbitt was making over $200 a week. That was a fortune.

LM: Have you talked to Art?

DJ: Yes, he's a crotchety old man.

LM: Probably very bitter. I'm sure he thought he was doing the right thing.

DJ: I know he did.

LM: Bob Martsch was an air-brush specialist.

DJ: When did he come to the studio? Was he there during _Snow White_?

LM: Yes. [Note: Bob Martsch joined on June 17, 1935.] ... We would pack their suppers and have picnics up on the hills on people's private property. We'd just walk on to private property, two couples of us, and have our picnics up there. And the husbands would go back to work again at the studio, at night. The girls would walk on home, [or] visit till the husbands got out about nine o'clock. They'd come walking home. This was in the thirties, while _Snow White_ was in production.

DJ: You didn't actually walk with your husband to work in the morning and then stay there all day.

LM: No, no, no. We met at dinner time and had picnics up on the hills around the old Hyperion studio.

[Walt] knew how to pick personnel. He was fantastic at the way that he could select the talent. Part of it intuitive. But also, I would think that it was that he recognized in other people things that he would like to be able to do himself and couldn't do. That [were] the things that he admired in other people. And these people were so loyal to him. There was a tremendous flow of loyalty in the studio, in those people. They stayed with him.

Al [Jones] was wonderful, open, gregarious. I think he was a technician. Very pro-union, which Walt was not. I think we met through a rock club at the studio, [and went] on trips like that. Josh would paint and sketch and we'd search for rocks and things on weekend excursions. Walt encouraged this sort of thing, too. We had this nice little room with machines set up to work over rocks and polish rocks.

DJ: And you would be doing this....

LM: At the studio.

DJ: While your husband was drawing the bubbles for _Snow White_?

LM: This was at night. Those were weekend and night-time activities, all sorts of things like that. Not during the thirties. This was at the new studio.

DJ: I know that on _Snow White_ they had a lot of overtime that no one ever got paid for ... but they all did it because they loved what they were doing.

LM: There was a bonus system. Josh got a bonus of a thousand dollars. There was never that much money in the _world_. Six hundred for the mural [and] a thousand dollar bonus on _Snow White_. We were invited to the party [at the Lake Norconian Hotel] and we got a thousand dollar bonus, too!

DJ: You were one of the lucky ones.

LM: It was according to your productivity. We did get the bonus on _Snow White_ and it was based on your production. Slave labor some of them may have called it. But if you produced, you got bonuses. I don't know who else got bonuses, but I do know that there were a number of them given. Different people mentioned it.

DJ: That was an astronomical sum in those days: a thousand dollars.

LM. A thousand dollars in cash, all at once?! Even in 1938, that was a lot of money. It was just before prices went up. They started escalating when the war in Europe [broke] out.

Interviewed on January 23, 1990.

Eustace Lycett (1914-2007)

During a 43-year career with Disney, starting in 1937, special-effects wizard Eustace Lycett worked on more than 30 films, from *Snow White and the Seven Dwarfs* (1937) to *The Last Flight of Noah's Ark* (1980).

In 1964, along with Peter Ellenshaw and Hamilton Luske, he won an Oscar for special visual effects for *Mary Poppins*. And in 1971, with Alan Maley and Danny Lee, he won another Oscar in the same category for *Bedknobs and Broomsticks*.

Eustace Arden Lycett was born in Straffordshire, England, on December 21, 1914, the son of Martha Constance Walley and William Arden Lycett. As a mining engineer, Mr. Lycett's father regularly moved with the family; they lived in Chile for years, and went to California in the early 1930s.

Lycett went to work for Disney three days after graduating from the California Institute of Technology in 1937 with a degree in mechanical engineering. He soon became a protégé of Ub Iwerks and worked on Disney's new multiplane camera.

In 1958, Lycett became head of the special photographic effects department.

His career there was not limited to the big screen. He helped design Great Moments With Mr. Lincoln, one of the most popular exhibits at the 1964–65 World's Fair in New York, and Rocket to the Moon, a major attraction at Disneyland.

Eustace Lycett died November 16, 2007.

David Johnson: How did you come to work at the Disney Studio?

Eustace Lycett: I graduated from Cal Tech in June of 1937. That was the last part of the Depression days and jobs were kinda hard to come by. A guy from Disney came over to Cal Tech looking for engineers.

DJ: Any particular kind of engineer?

LY: Mechanical engineer. Because they were designing.... Disney was in the middle of *Snow White*. They were trying to convert from the old Technicolor three-strip system to what they call a successive exposure system of photography. The old Technicolor camera used three films and it was a big cumbersome thing. We helped them design a new system there that was called successive exposure. See, if a cartoon doesn't move, you can take three pictures of a cartoon frame through the three different filters before you move on to the next frame. We would send that single black-and-white film to Technicolor and they would step-print from that. So I was designing equipment for that and also they were in the process of starting to develop the multiplane camera.

DJ: And you did that.

EL: I helped with that, yes. We had a little engineering department.

DJ: Did they actually have it built when you started working there?

EL: The original, the first one was built.

DJ: Do you know how old it was? A couple of months old?

EL: Yes, a few months old. At that time the multiplane was built, but it was the changeover to the successive exposure system which meant building a new camera and all that stuff.

DJ: They built a second multiplane. Was it during *Snow White*?

EL: During *Snow White* we just had the one multiplane, and at the time we were at the Hyperion studio. Then with the success of *Snow White*, Walt decided to build a big new studio out in Burbank. We were still at the Hyperion studio when we set to work designing a new and improved multiplane.

DJ: I'd like you talk about the multiplane camera and how it works— the early one, if you can differentiate between them.

EL: The second that we built was just a little bit more refined. But the original....

DJ: I know Garity designed it.

EL: Bill Garity was there and then Bill McFadden, who was the chief engineer under Bill Garity, was the guy that hired me. Then after

I got there they hired several other guys. Pretty soon we had about twenty people in the engineering department. The first multiplane camera was essentially a vertical camera that shot down with four vertical steel posts. Precision grounds to a post with racks under them. Then you could insert what we call levels in there. They were platforms that could move up and down. And the camera was on a platform that could also move up and down within these four posts.

DJ: Did the camera stay stationary? Could it move east-west?

EL: It could move east-west and north-south, but most of the panning action was done by moving glasses through the levels. There were three "background levels" and then there was an animation level, which had a platen on it, which could carry cels on the platen. The background levels were simple: all you could do was hold a piece a glass in those. But they all had east-west drives on them so that you could put a piece of glass in there and clamp it in there with a painting on it and they had counters that were calibrated in one-hundredth of an inch so you could sit there and you could move the glass one-hundredth of an inch each time, or more, if you wanted, but a minimum of one hundredth of an inch. So you could create a pan by moving the glasses. Then we would have four levels at a time and a couple of background levels and animation level and an overlay level.

DJ: I was told there were as many as six even in *Snow White*.

EL: No, we never had six

DJ: I meant six cel levels.

EL: Yes, six cel levels. That was the thing that we were constantly fighting is that these scenes would get so complex and the animation was so complex that the tendency was for the animators to ask for more and more cel levels. When you start piling up cel levels you get into all kinds of problems. First of all, the painting behind starts looking foggy, because four cels or more piled up.... And then the thickness or the difference between the top cel and bottom cel would be ... a little gap and you'd get shadows. So we used to try to persuade them to just use four cel levels, but on occasions we would have to give in and let them use six. Four cel levels was the standard. In fact, we'd carry four cel levels even in a scene when we had two working cel levels so that the density wouldn't change.

DJ: So the whole film was shot on four cel levels, basically.

EL: Basically four cel levels.

DJ: What were some of the problems and how were they worked out to get realistic pan movements? Like when Snow White goes into the forest. How was that calibrated so that you knew how fast the foreground would move in relation to the very far distance?

EL: Generally the layout man would design the scene. He would lay it out on a single level so if you'd have an overlay, a mid-animation level, and a couple of background levels he'd draw them all so that you could see the relationships. He'd just lay them on his table and you could see them all. When we put it on the crane, of course, we'd keep that same relationship and we'd have to reduce the overlay level and blow up the background level.

DJ: What do you mean by "reduce the overlay?" Make it smaller?

EL: Make it smaller, yes, if an animator designed an overlay, so when you put it on the camera that was all designed in one plane. Now, when you move that one up here fourteen inches there and the cameraman comes close that'll get bigger in the camera unless you reduce it, see. So we would make photostatic reproductions of the various levels. The lower ones we'd enlarge and the upper ones we'd reduce.

DJ: How much would you reduce them and how would you figure that out?

EL: By the camera lens and by whatever lens we were using. We had several different lenses on the camera. It was a 133mm lens that we used most of the time, and we knew exactly … because your main level was here and then fourteen inches up above … we had to keep the levels about fourteen inches apart, because we had to get light boxes in there to illuminate the levels. So, if you have a level fourteen inches apart there and your camera is up there and you're seeing this certain field on your main animation level, then it's very easy to calculate what field the camera will be seeing on this level up here. It would be smaller, because it's closer.

DJ: How do you make that calculation?

EL: It's just a matter of geometry. You just calculate the focal length with the lens and you know what the field is.

DJ: You make a triangle?

EL: We compiled a whole bunch of tables. Of course we used what we called fields. The main field is what they called a 6½ field. And usually these levels would be spaced about a field apart. It was about as close as we could get them and allow room for the light boxes. So you'd have 6½ field on the animation level, you'd have a 5½ field on.

That all had been calculated on tables so we knew exactly if this was fifteen inches above here that the camera was going to be seeing a 5½ field on this level, it'd be seeing a 6½ here and you'd be seeing a 7½ field down below and an 8½ field on the lower level. It was very easy. We could just calculate by the ratio. We just "ratioed" it and then, when we would take animator's original layout, we would reduce that proportionally on a photostat. Then we'd take that photostat and tape it to the back side of the piece of glass and the background man would paint the overlay.

DJ: Let's say you had a layout and Snow White is going through the forest here and you have all those trees and branches and stuff. Now, what if he wanted the foreground to be as large as the drawing. In other words, you made it smaller because....

EL: We made it smaller so that it would look like what the layout man had.

DJ: In other words, if you didn't make it smaller it would have looked bigger than on his drawing.

EL: Right. So in order to keep its relationships we had to....

DJ: Now, did you discover that right at the beginning or did you have to do a test before somebody saw that that was the case?

EL: That was pretty obvious that it would happen, and we knew that was going to happen, so we made up tables and then we would have these photostats and we'd tape those to the pieces of glass and give them to the artist and he would paint over those.

DJ: The upper level would move faster than the lower one?

EL: The upper level would *appear* to move faster.

DJ: Oh, I see, so you don't really move it faster.

EL: No, unless we wanted some kind of an unusual effect. Generally, if the thing was spaced out in a natural dimension, then we would move all the levels at the same speed, because there were larger fields on the bottom levels and small fields on the top level. The top levels would *appear* to move faster, just like in nature.

DJ: I had no idea. I always thought the upper level was actually being moved faster than the bottom level.

EL: No. That was just a natural. You had a predetermined field and you knew exactly what the camera was seeing. By moving at a fixed increment per frame, the upper levels would get across the field much sooner than the bottom levels, so they would appear to move faster.

DJ: So you might want to move it faster if there was a special [scene]?

EL: Oh yeah, we could re-proportion and, of course, there was no fixed rule. You worked things out. The normal rule was to move everything at the same speed, but there might be some situations…. And then, of course, we'd also truck the camera down, and you would have levels stacked up. What we see in *Bambi*, we start out and move in [and the same in *Snow White*]: you start down moving frame by frame. All of a sudden the camera gets up against the top level and you can't go any more. So they had to design it so that when the camera got where it was and couldn't go any further. You had to have clear glass on the top levels. You had to work out a field so that it would show … you get up there and you'd come through and you would know what field you had there and so you'd slip that level out and you'd slip a clear glass in the matte box in the camera to prevent any density change.

DJ: You'd keep the clear one on top going down all the time to keep the density.

EL: In other words we slip a glass in the matte box and keep on going down. Otherwise, the minute you took that level out you'd get a density change.

DJ: You said you've seen the film many times. Can you speak of some of the multiplane shots that you particularly remember?

EL: The famous scene where the dwarfs walked across the log. I remember working that out. That's how come I stayed with Disney because the multiplanes were built and there were engineering problems to be solved. At that time I was working with the animators and with the layout men on planning the multiplane. So we established another department called scene planning department. I had a couple of helpers and we'd get the animator's exposure sheet, which was the yellow exposure sheet that they animated [from], and we would make up another new exposure sheet called "multiplane exposure sheet" that had all the moves on and all the various levels.

DJ: I've got one here. That's from *Snow White*.

[...]

EL: The reason for double exposures in most cases was for what we call DX shadows, where you go through one exposure at sixty per cent with the shadow mask and then you go through the next exposure forty per cent without the shadow mask

[...]

The idea of using lacquer: I couldn't tell you where that came from or whose idea that was. It might have been [Leonard] Pickley's idea. Somebody came up with the idea of using lacquer and I think they experimented with it. It does produce a realistic looking ripple.

Another thing we had to watch out for is the background level. When you separated the levels, we had problems with reflections from one level to the other. And we used to black up the reflection. For a while there we had the guy do a base black before we painted anything. He would seal up the thing in black and then paint on top of it so that we'd have a black bottom, a black underside. Only in the painted areas. So that would reduce the problems of reflections. We had problems with reflections. We had to keep the light boxes low so that we could get the levels closer together and so the light had to come in at quite an oblique angle there. It was always a problem to get an even field. [This was corrected in the new multiplane.]

[Regarding frosted cel:]

It was an airbrushed cel that hadn't been fixed and then the animator would give the crane operator a guide and he'd put the guide on the pegs and they would tell him just how much to wipe off. [The residue may have been on another cel. It would have been very difficult to have done it with wipe-off alone. It was a very nerve-wracking process.]

There are several effects where you can use backlighting: double exposing stuff in sparkles on water and stuff like that. You shoot the scene first and then you come back and have a white card down below and a couple of cels moving each other with holes in them.

[Regarding backlighting:]

If the scene of *Snow White* holding the candle was done with backlight [and it was], you shoot the scene first with her holding the candle and no glow. Then you have one of the effects animators who would have animated a circle with a follow-through on a different cel. And then the whole cel would be painted black, leaving that area clear. Then you put your backlight and you stick the appropriate filter in the camera and then you use a heavy diffusion of some kind. Then you shoot the scene through again with just that one cel going on and that'll produce that effect. That's what we did on the "sugar-plum fairy" [sequence in *Fantasia*]. In other words, you'd just have a clear hole in a cel which has been keyed to the deal. And that hole would move around in exact sync with your drawing. As that hole moves around then you would add a color filter or whatever you're going to do and a heavy diffusion of some kind between the camera lens and that would produce.... We'd run tests to be sure until you got just the exactly right exposure that you wanted. Because if you hit it too hard you're going to burn out the thing. [On *Snow White*] if it flickered at all, it was air-brush.

[Regarding dx shadows:]

We shoot the scene through with a black cel over the character. Then you'd rewind the camera and come back and shoot the scene again with a less exposure without that effect.

[Regarding air-brush flickers:]

Now, if a lamp flickers and you know a candle flickers, you say, "Maybe it's all right for it to flicker." But if you want something with a steady glow that doesn't flicker then backlighting....

DJ: Would the glow from the backlighting project onto the figure here.

EL: Not unless you know.... On the second exposure, if you want that candle glow to go behind somebody you would then have to carry a mask of this guy, to keep the exposure from coming through. But if you didn't carry a mask there it would burn through.

DJ: The light from behind, how far would the light be?

EL: Usually it was just a white card.

DJ: So that's what you call a backlight?

EL: No, you put a white card and you light it and that way you can get even....

DJ: Oh, and then you place a piece of paper or cardboard on top of that with a little hole where you want it to go.

EL: That's right.

DJ: And if you diffuse that, then you could have a glow around it?

EL: That's right.

DJ: Can you have the lantern on one cel, on top of the glow, so that the lantern would be hard but the light would be kind of glowing.

EL: Right, yeah. You just carry a mask, or sometimes you turn the lights off on the animation level on that exposure so you can carry the cels as they're organized.

Sometimes it would take a couple of days [to make out the multiplane exposure sheet]. In the first place you have to figure out.... Now, you're going from 6100 to some other figure in so many frames, so you then have to calculate how [many] and then on top of that you've got to get what we call "slow in" and "accelerated in." You start slowing in and you build up speed. Then you'd have to regulate your constant speed to such a degree that you slow down and you arrive at the exact frame with a nice slow-up at the exact moment.

DJ: Was that trial and error?

EL: No, no. It was trial and error up to a point and we would come pretty close. We knew how much it would take, how many frames to accelerate and how many frames to decelerate. You'd run it and you go end up on the calculator and you might be off a few frames and then you'd make a few adjustments and you'd come out right on the frame.

DJ: So it would be safe to say nothing had to be re-photographed because of a miscalculation, or rarely?

EL: [That's right.] You were gradually building up speed [on slow-up into a truck]. But you were eating up frames and distance so you had to be careful if you had to calibrate the thing, so that when it is down at the other end you would arrive at the other end with the appropriate slow-up on the exact frame and the exact distances. Bill Garity was the chief engineer. He was kind of a big shot. Myself, Bill McFadden, and another guy named Jack [Keune?]. There were three of us. McFadden was a Caltech engineer. Lyle DeGrummond was head of scene planning before I became head of scene planning. He left the studio.

DJ: How many cameramen were there on the multiplane?

EL: We had two shifts on it. We used to run two twelve-hour shifts when we were getting toward the end of *Snow White*.

DJ: How many cameramen were on a shift?

EL: They had a standard production camera in the camera room and then they had a multiplane production camera. Three or four guys on the multiplane and then at least two guys on the standard plane.

DJ: The multiplane wasn't in the same room?

EL: Yes, it was [all in] one room.

DJ: Often they would shoot in the dark with these long exposures?

EL: The multiplane was over in one area and the standard camera was over here and the lights were pretty.... There were no overhead lights. The room lights were turned out and so you could run two cameras side by side.

DJ: So there were three or four on the multiplane and they worked twelve hours a shift?

EL: Twelve-hour shifts.

DJ: But that was only at the end of the thing. Was it in the beginning?

EL: Oh, no. Eight-hour shifts. When I first went there in 1937 we worked forty four hours a week. Half day on Saturday.

DJ: And what was your pay when you first started to Disney's?

EL: Thirty dollars a week.

DJ: How did you feel about the strike? You benefited from it?

EL: I had no part in the strike. I never struck. And the camera people never struck. It was the animators.

DJ: But because of the strike you got more money?

EL: As a result of the strike settlement, the camera department became part of the local 659.

DJ: $30 a week. Could you live on that?

EL: Oh, sure. You couldn't live handsomely, but I paid $25 a month rent. I was married and we paid $25 a month rent, and food cost about $10 a week.

DJ: You're from England?

EL: Originally.

DJ: What part?

EL: I was born in Stoke.

Interviewed in Winter 1988.

McLaren Stewart (1909–1992)

Layout artist McLaren Stewart was born on April 29, 1909, in Detroit, Michigan. He studied from 1927 to 1931 at the California School of Fine Arts and was hired by the Disney Studio on October 22, 1934. He soon started working as a layout artist on many of Disney's classic features up until *Bedknobs and Broomsticks* in 1971. He retired at some point in the 1970s and died May 14, 1992.

For *Snow White*, McLaren Stewart, one of the film's ten art directors (*i.e.*, layout artists) designed the entire "Heigh-Ho" sequence (beginning with the dwarfs leaving the mine), including its striking shadow-on-rock effect, the log-bridge, the witch's journey on foot to the dwarfs' cottage (including vultures), the animals' race to the mine, and their dash home with the dwarfs up to the witch's final chase.

David Johnson: How did you get to Disney's?

McLaren Stewart: It all boils down to the Great Depression. Although my parents were Canadian, I was born in Detroit and spent my early years in William, near Toronto. In 1915, when I was six, my family moved to San Francisco where I recall going to the World's Fair and watching some of the earliest bi-planes doing stunts, one of them crashing into a grounded "pusher plane."

I grew up in Alameda and later studied at the California School of Fine Arts in San Francisco (1927–31). I got out at a great time. I guess there's no good time for an artist to get out, but 1931 was just about as bad as it could be. So I tried to get into advertising art, but there was just nothing. I had a little studio up there and went around to see different people, trying to peddle my work, and [after 2 years] I wasn't even looking for an art job, just anything.

I finally went to see quite a well-known political cartoonist at that time in one of the San Francisco papers. I can't remember his name. I went in to see him to show him my work, and see if I could, who knows, just get anything. He happened to look at my things and amongst them I had a number of cartoon drawings. He said, "I have a friend who works down [at Disney's] and they're looking for people." This was in the summer or fall of 1934. "So," he said, "I'll give you a letter to go down."

I took his letter, thanked him, and managed to get a ride from San Francisco down to here and appeared at the studio one morning and handed the letter and the guy said, "You really should have just sent the letter and then we'll call you. But as long as you've come down here, why, we'll give you a chance." That was [director] Ben Sharpsteen.

[Since he seemed to have "potential," he was put into "training." This was a full week of basic ground work, mostly inbetweening in which the young recruits (eight to twelve men) learned the rudiments of animation. By Friday, those that "made it" began the following Monday, as inbetweeners, at $15 a week. The previous forty hours had all been "donated" time. "Max" and fellow artist Frank Teague were the only "graduates."]

[About story meetings]

They'd have the [story]boards up, [and you'd] come in, and everybody'd sit down and whoever was the storyman would get up and tell the story and it went along. Walt would stop, "Wait a minute. Hell, we're not goin' to do that!" And then we went through all this and there's an argument about that. And then if Walt liked it, "Well, OK," and if he didn't like it, BAM, BAM, BAM, BAM!, he'd pull all the pictures down and that's the end of that. So after the end of a story meeting, the floor would be littered with little drawings of what didn't pass. [During all this] the rest of us would sit around [and Walt would say,] "So what do you think? What do you think?" and so on. And we, [of course,] were all trying to make points by being bright and original, but Walt really handled the whole thing pretty much himself. He had used us to play ideas off of.... [As for wounded egos, there's really] nothing too personal about [all] that. Sure, you could be a little bit shocked—your artwork has been thrown on the floor. I've seen people argue with him. They never won.

[Disney's was] pretty much a one-man organization. Things weren't done by committee in those days, or rather with a committee with a chairman of the committee named Walt Disney. None of the mamby-pamby, should-we-do-this? type of thing done by committees [now]. I thought he was fair. I liked him.

[Walt's single-most important and brilliant contribution] was story. I've been in the business for a long time and I've never seen anybody else like him.

Interviewed on January 22, 1990.

Ken O'Connor
(1908–1998)

Ken O'Connor was a Disney layout artist par excellence for three-plus decades. He created images that became touchstones in our psyche, including the coach in *Cinderella*, the marching cards in *Alice in Wonderland*, and the dancing hippos in *Fantasia*.

As director T. Hee once recalled, "Ken was a charmer. Being from Australia, he'd make some crazy crack that only an Aussie can do. He was a bright, clever man and a man who enjoyed life. He never got upset about things, but just brushed them aside and kept on going. That made it nice for us to work together." Ward Kimball, who worked with Ken on many projects, including futuristic films for Disney television shows, added, "Ken arrived at some very interesting solutions. I'd ask him for some quick sketches of, say, how an underwater restaurant would look, and he would come up with some wild ideas."

Ken O'Connor was born in Perth, Australia, in 1908. He studied commercial art at Melbourne Technical College and fine art at the Australian National Gallery in Melbourne. He moved with his family to San Francisco in 1930, and continued his education there at the California School of Art.

In 1935, he joined Walt Disney Productions, staying with the company until his retirement in 1975. He was art director and layout artist for 13 feature-length animated films and almost 100 shorts.

During World War II, Ken worked on training and educational films that Disney produced for the U.S. government, including *Food Will Win the War*, along with theatrical cartoons such as *Education for Death*. Later, he provided layouts for the first 3-D cartoon *Adventures in Music: Melody*. He also served as art director on *Man in Space, Man and the Moon*, and *Mars and Beyond*, as well as the first CinemaScope cartoon *Toot, Whistle, Plunk and Boom*, which won an Academy Award in 1953. He continued to work with the company as a consultant for years after his retirement and was involved in the Universe of Energy at Epcot Center and the "Back to Neverland" history of animation film shown in the animation building at Disney-MGM Studios in Florida.

Upon his retirement from Disney, O'Connor pursued a second career: teaching a younger generation of artists at the Disney-created California Institute of the Arts in Santa Clarita.

Ken O'Connor died of pneumonia on May 27, 1998, at his Burbank home.

David Johnson: When did you come to America?

Ken O'Connor: I originally came in 1930.

DJ: Did you come to California?

KO: Yes. My father got a job as American representative for the Australian National Travel Association, which was federally sponsored. The fact that it was federally sponsored allowed him to bring his family in. The quota system was really tough then. Immigration was quite strict. But he was able to bring his family here, so that's how I was included, particularly as there were not a lot of artistic chances in Australia where I was born compared to America. We came to San Francisco and I started up there.

DJ: Where in Australia?

KO: We left from Sydney, but I was born in Perth, the capital of West Australia—although I left there when I was five, so I'm a little hazy on Perth. My dad thought it would be a nice idea to get arrangements for a twelve-month trip. The Australians all revered the old country [England]. Also he was a journalist and he owned a newspaper in Perth and he wanted to see Fleet Street in London ... the *London Times* and all these traditional things. So he thought it would be nice if the family spent twelve months there. I think to that end he got a job as secretary to the government of West Australia in London. And we were there and timed it just beautifully, because we went in 1914 and soon as we arrived they declared World War I. So we spent four years being bombed and starved and freezing. Houses didn't have any central heating or anything in those days. Snow on the ground outside the window was not my idea of a garden. Everything worthwhile was sandbagged up and you couldn't see the monuments and trees half the time. So then we went back to Australia in 1918.

Soon as they declared peace we went to the first boat to go back to the colonies. I stayed there most of the time. I also went to New Zealand for a while, and then I came to America.

DJ: How did you get to the Disney Studio, and when?

KO: I was an art director of a postal company in San Francisco, and I thought I was somebody being an art director. My dad, who was observant, said, "I have to go to southern California for two weeks," more or less for a vacation. And he said, "I think there's a river of gold running past that Disney Studio. Maybe you should go and see if you could join in." While in Australia and San Francisco I'd done a lot of cartoons and caricatures. I started off as a caricaturist in Australia. So I made up a little story and did the characters as well as I could, in color, and blew their noses and painted socks up and made it the best presentation I could. Having been in commercial art I knew how to doctor things up to sell and I just came down and applied. They very grudgingly admitted that I might be worth something.

DJ: Who did you see?

KO: The man I saw was called Ben Sharpsteen. He'd been an animator in New York and he had various positions there. He was a director when I got in and he was also an animation director at one time in the studio and probably the most feared man in the studio. He was a very tough man.

DJ: More than Dave Hand?

KO: Yes. Dave Hand was production chief, as I remember, then. He was important, but Ben was a very tough man. I knew because when I got in, I got into his unit and he was my director.

DJ: He also was the public relations for hiring?

KO: I don't think Walt knew what public relations were. He never had a very sympathetic feel toward that. He felt the product was so good it would sell itself. I submitted a portfolio and they looked at it and then Ben interviewed me and he admitted I might be of some use and so they gave me a tryout.

DJ: Do you remember what month and year this was?

KO: March of 1935. *Snow White* had started, but first I had to do a tryout. It was really terrible, actually.

DJ: What did you do?

KO: As I said, I had seen some animation, but I didn't know how it was done. I'd done still pictures and I didn't know an inbetween from a wheelbarrow. They had this entire room known as "the black hole," which was well named: an inside room, no windows, no air conditioning [in the] middle of summer. It was not very humorous trying to avoid sweating on the paper. Walt was busing in whole loads of artists, some of them quite prominent, from as far away as New York to tryout. So this square [room] was just the animation desk lights and otherwise black, and you attempted to do inbetweens. They gave you a scene and said, "Inbetween it." The first scene that I was supposed to inbetween was by Freddie Moore.

DJ: Do you remember what it was?

KO: It was a Mickey scene, that's all I remember. He was damn good on Mickey, too. But then I was told it was his roughs, and I couldn't believe it: they were so beautifully done. I didn't know what the hell else they could do to make it finished. Freddie was a natural, and almost a freak. He was so good. Anyway, I found out from the guy next to me what an inbetween was: you put down two extremes onto a light board and you put your paper on and you flip it and you draw in between. They told the guy next to me, "Here are the extremes, do something inbetween." So he pinned up the extremes up on the wall and he put paper on his desk and he'd look at the pair on the wall! He knew less than I did. That would be impossible. I mean if you're just told, "Now here're two drawings, now we want a drawing inbetween," they don't tell you how to do it. He didn't know about light boards and flipping and that. When I was in there the fellows were falling like nine pins, because half of them didn't know much or enough and they would after a while just take their coat off the back of the chair and leave, give up. It was very tough. I inbetweened it reasonably successfully. I was criticized for how I inbetweened the bow tie or something that went up to down. There's a way of doing a curve on an inbetween and I didn't know. I just made a real literal geometric inbetween and got bawled out. But they thought I might have promise, so then I was put in the inbetween department, which was not a lot better, because they had a very nervous neurotic chap running it.

DJ: George Drake.

KO: And he was a fearsome man. He was erratic. If he didn't like the way you brushed your hair (I had a little hair then), you'd liable to be out on your head. Anyway, he ran it, and I lasted two weeks on that, and then they put me in special effects animation under a Chinaman, Cy Young. So a Chinaman was teaching an American thing to an Australian, and we got pretty involved. He had a theory, a formula for everything, and I learned a lot from him. Although what I got sentenced to was awful.

It sounds like I'm doing nothing but complain, but I think the first thing they gave me was in *Three Orphan Kittens* where a kitten knocked over a pepper pot. The pepper went up in the air and it all had to come down, and so three of us were sitting in a row animating clouds of pepper. You went like this with a pencil.... So it sounded like three woodpeckers all day long: bang, bang, bang ,bang, bang! Really a thrilling experience. Thank god mine worked. You didn't literally follow every little dot through: you got the general mass to go down. Not my idea of a creative effort. In fact I was sort of irritated that they suggested that I wasn't Michelangelo and I had to prove myself. And here I had had ten guys working for me in San Francisco at the parcel company. I thought I was a leading character, and I found out in a hell of a hurry that I wasn't.

Timing is the difference, you see. Posters and caricatures, any of that stuff, commercial art: it's all the reader determines, how long they look at the thing before they turn the page. Here with the time stuff, limited footage and different speeds, you had to know how fast to animate the thing across the screen. If it's going slowly it took so many drawings, and faster, less drawings and so forth. It was a whole art that I wasn't familiar with, and it really took months before I really was of good use to the company, even though I was a draughtsman. I could draw. That didn't count until you learned the technique of motion and time. Timing was a whole big thing you ran into. If you'd been an easel painter or anything like that, you didn't have to think in those terms.

DJ: What was your pay at the time?

KO: Probably about $75 a week, I imagine.

DJ: That's not too bad.

KO: When I started off in inbetween it was $15 a week. Girls were getting $18 a week: competent inkers and painters. I didn't see how they could stay respectable at that. I had a family behind me and some savings from my previous job, which all sort of enabled me to float along, because even for those days that was pretty low. Then in the first year I got seven raises. They weren't very big raises, but I got up to maybe a hundred dollars, something like that. I was becoming a star. I remember envying Charlie Philippi and these good men: they got a $150 a week. Layout men [like] Hugh Hennesy and Charles Philippi and Tom Codrick. Wonderful artists, much better than the average animator, incidentally.

DJ: Did they get bonuses, too?

KO: At that time, yes. Walt had a paternal feeling, and if there were profits he cut up a melon, as they said, at the end of the year, and gave some of us bonuses. I didn't get them right away, because I was first a lowly inbetweener and I worked up.

DJ: Going back to the special effects: how long were you in Cy Young's department?

KO: Not very long. It could have been about six months. I got a great opportunity. They needed somebody to do rotoscope.

DJ: Would this have been towards the end of 1935 that you were put to this task?

KO: Yes, because ultimately I was rotoscoping in *Snow White*, which was released in 1937. I wasn't very long in Special Effects. I'd probably have stayed there except for this great opportunity.

DJ: Did you ask to change out of FX?

KO: No. I had my eye on Layout all the time, because I had done commercial layout and I could see that…. I'd spent years in learning. I'd done oil painting, I'd done rendering of all sorts in commercial art, and I spent a lot of time learning how to draw and render in paint and so forth. Animation is linear, almost exclusively line drawings of the character. In other words, you have to be an actor, and that's the important thing. I'm not putting it down: it's important to be a good actor and a versatile actor, because you have to handle different characters. But I wanted Layout, because I saw that I could conceive a scene best at the start, and if necessary to render it in values, or render it in color to give the background people a good start when they start painting it and so on. I studied rather widely, because I'd been to our National Gallery in Melbourne in Australia and commercial art schools and fine art schools in San Francisco by then, and I didn't want to throw that rendering ability away. So I didn't want to get into animation as such. It just had to be a stepping stone, and I never had rotoscoping in my concept at all, because that is not creative, in my view.

DJ: Right. I'm just wondering why they threw it at you.

KO: They just wanted to find someone who could trace off accurately and they were just trying me out to see if I'd work. I made a ghastly mistake, tactically, because the rotoscope machine was very primitive. It was an animation desk with a glass panel, and they had a two-by-four running down to the ground of the floor. On that they had a little magic lantern thing, like a light that projects still-frame film. So you put the film in that on a certain frame and you turned the light on and then you went to the desk and the light projected up, and then if you had to have the image at a certain size or enlarging it or something, you pulled a piece of string, you pulled the magic lantern up the two-by-four and that made the image get smaller. Or you let it down, and when you get the right thing you tie it up with string ... this is high tech. You see how primitive it was. So that was the idea. Then you got the right size.

They gave me first a sample scene and when I looked at it I nearly had an attack, because the scene was a little over a half-an-inch high. That's how big they wanted it. It would be animated big, photographed on film, and they wanted it this size. It was of a judge rapping on a stump with a gavel, and every time he hit the gavel there's a book about an eighth-of-an-inch wide on the stump, and it jumped up and opened, and all the pages opened and fell back. It was so small I could hardly see what the hell I was doing. But they suggested that I mightn't be the greatest artist in the world, and so I was determined to show them.

I rigged a high-powered magnifying glass on the stand and a 9H pencil, which is like drawing with a needle, and sharpened the devil out of it. I engraved every frame so that when that little book opened up if you looked close enough you'd see all the pages open and so forth. The whole damn scene was that big. I thought, you know, I'll show them I got good eyes, at least. They didn't know I was using a magnifying glass. So I did that, and Fergie [Norm Ferguson] came in to flip it and he flipped it and the closer he looked, God, the more detail in this thing. He said, "God, this guy's a genius at this. What eyes he must have!"

We always used five field then. We hadn't got up to six field. All the crowds and bugs and everything were done at that small scale. But this was worse. See, this judge in *Who Killed Cock Robin?* was down at the end of a whole bunch of people, so he had to be small. I'm sure the audience looked at the people and it was absurd how accurately and how detailed I did it. But Fergy got so impressed that he said, "Hey, this is the guy." So then they said, "You do all the rotoscoping in *Snow White*," which is exactly what I didn't want. I said, "Damn it, I'm creative." Anyway, they sentenced me to that, and so I had a room to myself totally black except for the light on the board, and I started up and they photographed the girl for *Snow White*, [Marjorie] Belcher. Anyway she did the action and I traced off, god knows how many [frames], maybe a couple of hundred a day, frame after frame. And I was really getting fed up.

DJ: Do you remember what scenes these were, the very first ones that they asked you to trace?

KO: I did masses of scenes. These things were like she was horsing around in the kitchen by the sink, the pump, and doing the dishes. She was acting it out and didn't have all the props, and talking to the animals, tidying up the house.

DJ: Was this black-and-white film or was it in color?

KO: Black and white.

DJ: Do you remember doing the scene where she goes through the forest?

KO: Charlie Philippi laid that out. I did [the rotoscoping on that]. In that case Charlie Philippi and the director worked out very short scenes, only eight frames a scene or something where she came up, or the eyes would come out of the tree. I admired what he had laid out, and they shot the live action to his layouts. Charlie Philippi was damn good. He was one of my teachers, he and Hugh Hennesy and to some extent Tom Codrick, although I was officially under another layout man, a man you hardly ever hear [of]. He wasn't a very well-known layout man. But I looked up and admired these other fellows and asked questions and they were very good, I thought.

DJ: Going back a bit, do you think anything influenced Philippi in his design of laying out the forest sequence?

KO: I'd say undoubtedly he went by storyboards. The story department and story sketch men put down general impressions and he cut it into scenes and decided on good angles, improved the staging. The layout man's function is to stage a picture. He, I'm sure, stepped up the storyboard quite a lot, because that was his function. But he undoubtedly started from the storyboard.

I always thumbnail before I do the rough layouts, and discuss that with the director. I only know that Charlie would have improved whatever he got. The function of the layout man is to look at the damn storyboard with or without the director and see any weaknesses and see new angles to look at the thing from: closer, longer, up-shot, down-shot, rotate the camera, and get camera mechanics into it that the story sketch man doesn't have to. He just has to put over the story points. Charlie wasn't too talkative. He would just sit there and chew gum and smoke cigarettes, which he stopped one day just like that, and I admired that. Then I said, "Don't you miss those cigarettes?" "No." And he smoked all the time!

Anyway, when I first went here, he was laying out the well stuff where she was down sweeping and so forth, with the pigeons. He was doing it beautifully, just sort of out of his head. He had a great way of drawing everything, trees and god knows what, anything. The whole [animation studio] was like an assembly line. Each person had a function and each person was supposed to plus everything they got. That was the key thing with Walt. You don't minus anything, you plus everything. When the person in the layout and the director get together they look at the story. It's okayed by Walt, but they don't take it as final. Anything they can see to tighten up the story or improve it, they do. And that was his principle: everyone was supposed to plus everything all along the line. It didn't always work, but it was a basic doctrine that was driven into us, and we always tried to do it. It was a large reason for Disney quality.

DJ: Did you have model sheets to work with when you did rotoscoping?

KO: Absolutely not. Before Snow White, I had done a little bit of rotoscoping. After I had made my tactical error and was put permanently on rotoscope, where they would animate Mickey skating toward you with some sort of crack in the ice ... he was just on one size, but on rotoscope I made him get bigger. I put the truck in. As I traced I put the thing back and the image got bigger and lining things up. So when I finished with it he was skating toward you. The animator just had to do two steps, one size, side-to-side, then I followed through.

DJ: Did the director tell you they wanted that?

KO: Yes, I was told they wanted a truck, and they wanted to get this big, and then I would pro-rate certain images. I'd done things like that that weren't just plain tracing, although I had to trace them each time. On *Snow White*, they just sat the girl and I had black-and-white film of her running around dancing, doing whatever she did, falling down, crying, whatever, and I just did her. If there was a pan, if she ran a long way, they put sticks on the stage at intervals, so that I'd trace the sticks so they knew how far she ran. Then the animator knew how far and how fast to move the background behind her.

DJ: Were you there when they photographed her?

KO: No, I wasn't.

DJ: So they used sticks actually on the soundstage.

KO: They had sticks on little squares of wood as they went by. And she ran in one place, because the camera was following her. So you knew how fast to move the background behind it. It might be trees or rocks or anything. This was a good guide to the layout man and everyone, how long to lay out the pan.

DJ: Do you know who thought of that?

KO: That was done early on, before I was conscious of what happened there. I think it was almost right at the start of *Snow White*. We didn't normally shoot before *Snow White*.

And in answer to your other question: I needed no model sheets. I just took her and the sticks, and that's it. But I did her carefully and that's all I did, in outline. That was given to the animator. He then changed her proportion, [gave her] a bigger head, changed her into Snow White. That gave the animator timing. That's the main thing: how long does it take her to do everything. If she did a good performance in acting he'd follow that pretty closely, but if he thought again that it could be better, he'd plus it. He'd hold a little longer when she held or he'd move her quicker. That was the animator's privilege. Here he had a good performance on film that he'd run on his moviola and he could also look at the tracings I had on the board, put his paper over, and if he went with it, he'd just change the proportions. And if there was any costume change he would add that and he'd observe if he shot a test too fast to move the background behind her for so many feet. It was very helpful to him, I'm sure, but I just disliked it intensely because it wasn't creative.

DJ: How long were you doing this?

KO: I went for maybe about six months on the things. The amusing thing for me was that I was about to resign, because I said, "This isn't creative. I'm a creative person and I'm doing nothing but trace. Not only that, I don't see the light of day all day, except for a short lunch, and I don't find this inspiring." And one day Walt came in and he maneuvered all over the plant and he looked over my shoulder, and I was thinking how I'd tell him I'm going to lay off this which is no good. But I didn't say anything, luckily. He said, "Boy, are you lucky!" And I began to think how lucky I'd tell him I thought I was, being sentenced to this. I made some non-committal reply, and then he launched into a thing. He said, "Look, the animators have action analysis classes where we put the stuff on a frame at a time so we can see how a horse sits down or a cow gets up or a man runs or whatever. But they only get that for a short time as a part of the school in the week. You're getting it fired at you all the time, a chance to analyze human action."

He really got me so steamed up, you know. I realized I was wrong. I should have been analyzing it, because on human action there's a lot of anticipation and follow through in all the motions, and I'd been just doing it mechanically. Carefully but mechanically, and not studying how Snow White was anticipating before she did something, and when she did something how much follow-through there was. Anyway, it was very instructive, once I got the hang of what he was talking about. I realized that I should have been studying this, the human action, which is the most difficult action to study that there is. I saw that this guy could sell ice boxes to Eskimos, if he could sell me on rotoscoping. So I went out twice as hard, but I still really wanted to get out of it, into Layout.

DJ: Did you do only Snow White or did you do some of the queen?

KO: No, I didn't, because, as far as I remember, I succeeded in getting into Layout. See, in those days they used to give you four or five dollars for any gag you could come up with, so I'd trace in the daytime and go home, think up gags, and render them and submit them. My gags weren't necessarily great, but I rendered the devil out of the drawings so they were done by Rembrandt, hoping I'd catch the eye of somebody who'd say, "Maybe this guy can draw." And that's what happened.

I submitted a lot of them and it caught somebody's eye and they said, "Maybe this guy can draw," and so they gave me a shot first at story sketch. I was still aching for Layout. The story sketches were OK and then I got a chance to.... Leo Seally was the name of the layout man I was put under. He was an old-time newspaper man, and I worked with him on a couple of shorts, on memorable shorts like *Mickey's Circus*.

DJ: When you were in Story Sketch then you weren't doing any *Snow White* at that time. That was for shorts.

KO: We made shorts at the same time we made features. There was a flow of shorts going through all the time. One layout man would handle six shorts at a time when he was a shorts layout man.

Interviewed in 1988.

Claude Coats (1913–1992)

Claude Coats' fame as a Disney color stylist and concept designer is second only to Mary Blair's.

Born on January 17, 1913, in San Francisco, California, Coats graduated from the University of Southern California, in 1934, with an architecture and fine arts degree. He began his career with Disney in June 1935, after studying at the Chouinard Art Institute. As a background painter at the Disney Studio, he contributed to the background and color styling of most Disney animated features, from *Snow White and the Seven Dwarfs* to *Lady and the Tramp*.

In 1955, Coats joined WED Enterprises (now Walt Disney Imagineering). A key designer from Disneyland's inception, Coats created attraction concepts like Mr. Toad's Wild Ride, Pirates of the Caribbean, Haunted Mansion, the Grand Canyon and Primeval World dioramas, and Submarine Voyage. When Walt Disney created show pavilions for the 1964 New York World's Fair, Coats was at the center of Magic Skyway, Carousel of Progress, and It's a Small World. He also helped create numerous attractions for Epcot Center, including World of Motion, Horizons, and several World Showcase pavilions.

Claude stood six feet, 6-1/8 inches tall. He recalled how Walt used to kid him about his height: "When the Disneyland Stagecoach was completed at the studio, Walt and a driver were giving rides around the lot, but he wouldn't let me get in. He said I spoiled the scale."

After 54 years with The Walt Disney Company, Coats retired from Walt Disney Imagineering on November 30, 1989. He died of cancer in Los Angeles on January 9, 1992.

David Johnson: Were you from California?

Claude Coats: Yes, born in San Francisco, but I went to school here in L.A. I took architecture and fine arts at USC. I graduated in fine arts, because I became more interested in the art end than in the engineering end.

DJ: What was your first assignment [at Disney] before *Snow White*?

CC: I worked on some of the cartoons. I started out as an apprentice. Just did little pieces of things: cutouts, overlays. I think I did some shingle roofs for *Mickey's Fire Brigade*, something like that.

DJ: Did you go into the studio to be hired as a background painter?

CC: Yes.

DJ: When you first started on *Snow White*, do you remember some of the first backgrounds that you did?

CC: Yeah, the first section I worked on was that "Wash Your Hands" [with the] soap.

DJ: Did you do the one with the big bar of soap that the fly is on?

CC: Yeah. And I had that little section by myself at first. And then the castle stuff came along and I did a lot of the castle things [like] Snow White at the well. Hugh Hennesy and Charlie Philippi did a lot of the things and Ken Anderson was getting going in there.

DJ: Do you know who painted that [the opening castle shot]?

CC: Probably Sam Armstrong. He was the lead painter, background artist.

DJ: Can you recall who designed the magic mirror with the zodiac?

CC: No, probably that same layout group.

DJ: Did you paint this one?

CC: No, I don't think I painted that one. I painted this one.

DJ: Oh, the one with Snow White at the beginning. Did you do the painting on glass for the multiplane?

CC: Some of that, yes.

DJ: So you did all of that beautiful pastel stuff.

CC: Yeah.

DJ: I was told that Sam Armstrong was the one who was kind of responsible for toning down the colors. Is that correct?

CC: Yeah.

DJ: Was that his idea or was it Walt's idea?

CC: I don't know. I think it probably was ... he kind of developed a formula so that everyone could paint them and they all looked the same. That's why sometimes it's very hard to know whether you painted the background or not. Like the little cottage was all painted in grey, Payne's grey, watercolor, painted on Whatman paper. And he had a certain way of doing the plaster wall in Payne's grey. Then he tinted them with something else. So this is watercolor, it looks a little grainy sometimes.

DJ: Now, your procedure, as a water colorist: would you do the darks first?

CC: No, usually, kind of the lights first and then going dark to darker. I always work in acrylic now. In fact, I'm trying to get up the nerve to try some watercolor again. They're tricky.

DJ: Did you happen to do this one? [Witch with apple.]

CC: Yeah.

DJ: How long would it take you to do a background like this one?

CC: I don't know, probably a day or two days. I think Ray Huffine was the artist who did a lot of this section. [Queen with peacock throne.]

DJ: I'm wondering who might have designed this throne?

CC: I would guess Hugh Hennesy, but I wouldn't know for sure.

DJ: You didn't do the huntsman? How about in the woods?

CC: No, I didn't do any of that. A lot of those [forest trees] were in oil for some reason. Stark Davis [did this], but I don't think he's listed either.

DJ: Why were they in oil?

CC: I think he just liked to work in oil and it had a little different feeling about it anyway.

DJ: But most of the others were watercolor backgrounds?

CC: Yes. I didn't do any for "Whistle While You Work." I did a little bit of the stuff in the mine. There were a lot of people working on that. I did some in the house, but not an awful lot. In the cottage.... The one with the mist, she's in the boat.

DJ: Was that shot with a scrim in front of it?

CC: No, a cel as I recall, with airbrush on it.

DJ: Did they tell you that you could do pretty much what you wanted to do? [Referring to above scene.]

CC: No. The layout people really suggested the mood.

DJ: But would they suggest the color to you? Ken O'Connor said that sometimes he would suggest what the colors were, but he said that the background painter didn't have to follow it; that he could do what [he wanted].

CC: It's kinda that way. And lots of times we'd make a.... I liked to do an isolated light thing, real lighting sometimes. I'd always find [a way to] create a piece of space for the character to animate in.... Kind of make a little island of light. ... They usually have tracer people to trace things. They take the layout and trace it on a piece of Whatman board. At that time we stretched the paper.

DJ: How could you stretch a paper without breaking it?

CC: You get it wet. Watercolorists used to always do that and put it on a piece of Masonite and tape it down while it's wet. Then when it dries out, it's under tension, so when you wet it, it doesn't curl and crinkle.

DJ: What kind of paper did you use?

CC: I think it was probably Whatman paper. But it was a kind that wouldn't have a lot of tooth to it. Because a lot of tooth would show up on the screen. And after a while we began using illustration board.

DJ: Was that for *Snow White* or afterwards?

CC: It was maybe even during that time. Afterwards I know we used it, because sometimes it would curl up and fall off the table at night.

DJ: Was it cloth, rag paper?

CC: It was probably regular watercolor paper. ... This section I think was Art Riley who was working at MGM, kind of helped us do the artwork. He worked then for the studio for a long while.

DJ: You mean the one of the witch going through the countryside.

CC: Yeah, and the escape scene and up to the lightning and the rock and all of that.

DJ: Now the size that you used for the backgrounds.... What was the smallest size? Would that be a four-field size?

CC: Yeah, sometimes we would get down that small, especially on trucks, where you wanted to get down close or something. But on [most of the stuff] it was done on a five-field. On the experimental picture, *The Old Mill*, I think they went to 6½.... Of course most of the industry uses a different peg system.

DJ: So some of the backgrounds were painted on the five field size.

CC: Most of them were larger.

DJ: Do you remember how large were the largest sheets you would use for *Snow White*? Could they be larger for pans?

CC: Yes, when we got into the big multiplane scenes, they might have been large. That's why we'd paint [them] on glass, most of them.

DJ: Did you do any of those scenes that would have been on the multiplane?

CC: Yes. You know, it just might have been a moving cel. The foreground. I would have painted that.

DJ: Did you paint any of the long pans? For instance, there was one pan that shows Snow White down here at the balcony and they pan up to the queen?

CC: Yes, that's in the hallway too [at the studio].

DJ: Did you do that one?

CC: Yeah.

DJ: Because that's faded. I believe it was Hugh Hennesy's layout. It was done in red pencil.

CC: I think that was probably Sam Armstrong. Usually whoever styled the picture usually kept control of how it looked, by hitting the high spots, and then other people would follow that lead.

DJ: Sam Armstrong was the head background man, you would say?

CC: Yes, and there was a kind of ... right in the middle of everything ... you know, Mique Nelson was really the head of the background department and he really wanted to style this picture, but I guess Walt wanted Sam to do it.

DJ: How were they different and how do you think Nelson would have done it?

CC: He wasn't as a good an artist as Sam.

DJ: How did Nelson want to do it?

CC: He had been an earlier painter for shorts. And they were simple. They didn't have that life in them, that feeling of what is real. Walt wanted a lot of effort into this picture. And we put a lot of time in on it.

DJ: Do you think Nelson would have wanted a more cartoony [approach], more bright colors?

CC: Yeah.

DJ: Did he ever tell you this personally?

CC: No. He was really a newspaper artist and he wasn't really a strong painter. Sam Armstrong was a really good painter.

DJ: Were all of the artists in the same room together?

CC: No, at the time they were scattered around. After a while, because they got so big, the apartment was filled up. Sam Armstrong had probably about eight desks along up to the window.

DJ: Were you in his office?

CC: That's where I started. No, he had his desk in the same office, and then when I got working on the castle it was a little different. There hadn't been too much done on it, and I think I went to some other room and I didn't need to be in the same [room].

DJ: When you say somebody would trace the layout onto this paper, how detailed would they trace it?

CC: We always had the layout crew that would come up and [draw it in]. It was just kind of a guide.

DJ: Would this be an assistant background painter or would this be an assistant layout person that would do this tracing?

CC: I think we had tracers at that time.

DJ: And he would do it very lightly in pencil

CC: Yeah. No, I think we didn't do that. I guess we just did our own or something.

DJ: Do you remember any of the background paintings you did for _Snow White_ that were particularly difficult, that gave you problems, or maybe had to be done over?

CC: No, I can't think of any. Have you run across Phil Dike's name?

DJ: Oh, yes.

CC: He was the one who hired me and he never painted too many backgrounds, even though he had a screen credit. He usually didn't paint any backgrounds, but he sort of did a lot of the color work, for Technicolor and stuff. Walt had really got him in through his search to get in some other artists. I think Walt was already kind of dissatisfied with Mique Nelson. He thought the quality he needed for this picture wasn't there. And so, that's why he wanted to try out _The Old Mill_.

DJ: You were talking about Phil Dike.

CC: I had been exhibiting watercolors around in different shows, and he was really a fine-art painter. He's from Redlands. I don't think I ever met him [before Disney], but he knew my work and some guy—I guess it was a mutual friend—said, "Go out and see him," and he gave me some other problems to do, like do something else out of a … to see what else I could do. And I did several trial things and finally they had an opening in the background department and he put me in with him. While he didn't do any paintings, he was helpful in suggesting things and he might have even suggested the mood. I'm not positive. He did handle the Technicolor quality of the final prints that we got back. And he was at the studio maybe four or five years.

DJ: The backgrounds you did for _Snow White_: When you saw them on the screen…. First of all, did you see any of it, like in a color test, before you actually went and saw the premiere?

CC: Oh yeah, we'd always see dailies.

DJ: Were they in color?

CC: Oh yeah. You know how the progression goes: from the rough thing and sometimes the storyboards are even done. But as you go, finally there's a cleanup reel and then finally when the prints came back, we'd always…. It was in the afternoon, and usually Walt would come in, and if he saw something he didn't like or a director saw something he didn't like, usually they were done over (like some camera mistake or cel not painted right in a flash or something like that). [But] usually things were pretty well established ahead of time. In fact, we might have done an early reel on a picture with just the high spots, so that everyone knew of what the flavor was going to be.

DJ: How did the color look on the Technicolor print that you were watching [in the dailies] compared to the color that you did? What was your reaction?

CC: Sometimes you get a little fooled because of the density of the cels. Cels do make a difference and grey things down a little bit. As I remember, the thing quite often went darker than we expected it to.

DJ: Do you recall if the yellows were true to your original painting or the reds were true? Or were you terribly disappointed, saying "No, that doesn't look like my painting at all."

CC: Sometimes that would happen, and that would be the time that Phil Dike would have to get an answer print. The first prints, the dailies, were not always true color. It was kind of an interesting job to know what was painted and to correct it in the answer print. I guess they make a note in the final answer print: they can dial in more color or less color and adjust it that way.

DJ: What was your favorite background?

CC: I know [Gustaf] Tenggren did a drawing of the little dwarfs crossing a log. A shadow comes up and they cross a log. [Note: Tenggren did not show the shadow. That was the invention of layout man Max Stewart.]

DJ: Oh yes, did you paint that background?

CC: That's the drawing. I kind of think I did. And that might have been multiplane. I'm not real positive.

DJ: That was multiplane.

CC: I was working on some part of it. One thing at the premiere that I think was really a very satisfying thing was that there was a lot of applause, just highlights in the picture. And a lot of them were surprised that people reacted so well to water reflections or like the mood scene, because I think people didn't expect so much mood out of a cartoon picture. They were thinking they were just going to be [seeing] the usual run of things. Quite often there would be applause about the girl running through the forest or something like that, and people were just reacting to what was a surprise to them, the beauty of things. It might have been one of the real surprises of *Snow White* … unless they'd seen *The Old Mill*, which had a lot of flavor to it. But up until then, things were just kind of … do it so fast, you know. Cartoons were always so quick that there's hardly any chance to get into a big mood section on things.

I think I liked the bar of soap. And that whole section. One of them is printed in one of the books and it's called a scene out of *Pinocchio*!

DJ: Did you paint that one?

CC: Yeah. Another book came out [*Treasuries of Animation Art*] and for some reason they keep saying "artist unknown." If they had just asked for an hour of Ken O'Connor and some of mine or John Hench's time, they could have identified, I think, all of them. But that's kind of a silly thing to put on something: "artist unknown." Backgrounds are kind of odd, because of us painting the same theme, you might say, from a different angle, or a different reason. Or sometimes a different animator would frame something a little different. Maybe this time he has the guy walking a little higher, so there's got to be two backgrounds for it, but it had to look the same. It's very difficult always to be sure, especially after all [these years].

That was such a real good period in Disney's history, because everyone had their fingers crossed for that thing. They knew their whole future rested on how that picture went over and it went over so well. That's where all the money came in to build the studio. Walt was always good about…. He made what he called a salary adjustment after all the money had been coming in. Kind of a bonus system. He called it a salary adjustment and then he gave everybody more money.

DJ: When you first began working at Disney's what was your salary?

CC: Fifteen dollars.

DJ: Most of them were $15 a week. I guess that was the standard.

CC: My wife made sixteen when she started, because there was some kind of state law that that was the minimum for women. Walt had been kind of burnt by Ub Iwerks taking a lot of the people away.

So even if we got around about $30 [a week], we got contracts or something like that. It didn't seem to make any difference. I had a three-year contract and it was supposed to be $30, but Walt was good about [that]. I still had the contract for $30 but I was making $150, which was pretty darn good in those days, just before the strike. Then finally I got a new contract. But he did things like that that he didn't have to do. He talked a lot about putting in a swimming pool at the studio, but he never did it. He did put in a putting green, but they found out it was too hard to maintain, so we played croquet on it.

DJ: Were you present at any of the live-action shootings, like the huntsman or Snow White?

CC: No. Maybe I looked in on Belcher in there, on the soundstage out of curiosity. ... Art Riley did the backgrounds for the chase scene [for the finale.] I think probably Sam Armstrong painted those.

DJ: I know that Sam Armstrong painted the castle in moonlight. I saw his name on that one. Did you go to any of the story meetings on *Snow White*?

CC: No. In fact, I was working on cartoons at first, and I really began to hear that there was a feature going on. There wasn't much publicity about it.

DJ: Once you got on the picture were you pretty much on it?

CC: Yes, pretty much on it, and I think Mique Nelson kept the cartoon things going. Actually, we finished the backgrounds early, before the inking and painting was done, so I painted on a lot of the cels. There was this big, frantic crush to get the thing finished, and so we were working overtime. We moved to another room or something and the girls were way into it. They'd just tell us what to do. That lasted for a couple of weeks, but it was just a big, frantic effort to get the thing done.

DJ: How many actual separate backgrounds did you paint yourself for *Snow White*? Would you say it was between seventy five and one hundred? Or not that many?

CC: I don't have any idea. I suppose six or eight people were on it and Ray Huffine. I thought he would have been on it, but maybe not. Maybe Ray Lockrem was the one who did those thrones. He did a lot of the stuff on *Old Mill*.

Sam was working on *Snow White* and Mique Nelson and myself moved to another room and we did shorts for a while. Then, I think that washing sequence came, all in a bunch, and I did that and the castle stuff. I was with Mique Nelson on the shorts, and I got a lot of experience then, because his eyes were getting bad and he didn't do an awful lot of work.

DJ: What about Sam Armstrong. What was he like?

CC: He was a very quiet man. He probably was in his 40s, I guess. To me he was kind of an elderly figure. Same with Mique Nelson. I became very good friends with both of them. In fact, I was kind of caught in the middle, because they began to have quite a feud going.

DJ: During *Snow White* or after?

CC: I don't know. And finally I think Mique Nelson was let go.

DJ: What was the feud about?

CC: It probably started from the fact that Mique Nelson had been in charge of the background department and now Sam Armstrong had the plum picture and was really in charge of it. I remember I worked with Mique on another one of the wolf pictures, and we did several others, and then finally when Mique left then I.... Did Merle Cox get a credit?

DJ: Yes, for *Snow White*.

CC: He and I did a short together, one that had all those bottles in it: *Three Blind Mouseketeers*.

DJ: The department got divided?

CC: Yes, Sam and Ray Lockrem and some people he'd been working with on *The Old Mill* started early on *Snow White* and that's why a lot of the first section, I believe, was things like the dwarfs' cottage.

DJ: Those were the first backgrounds?

CC: I think so, yes. They finally had a lot of that underway and then when things like the washing sequence came in then they took me out of shorts. There probably were no shorts being made. They were just pushing to get the feature out.

DJ: So it's fairly safe to say that once you got onto *Snow White*, you stayed on it, for the better part of a year and a half.

CC: Probably. It's a wild guess, but I think about a year and a half or so.

DJ: And all the work you did was watercolor or did you gouache?

CC: Might have been some of those things painted on cel looked liked it might be oil, a branch that might have been a cel, or might have been a paper cut out. Sometimes we did those. I'm sure the posts [at the wishing well] were paper cutouts. And sometimes those would be on a separate cel, and they never liked to use really more than four cels. The pigeons are probably on one cel and the girl's on another. And sometimes for different reasons, they would maybe get five cels.

DJ: I know they used up to six, rarely.

CC: Then it usually gets a little milky and does something to the color. If you knew that ahead of time, and you did, you always knew what would be on it, because usually you had a cel setup to work from.

DJ: What is a cel setup?

CC: You would get a model cel, especially if it was a different coloring or a night scene or anything like that. And we would work with the color-model people. Sometimes the animators would have ideas about what the color would be, and sometimes the layout men would, too. Of course your story dictated what kind of a night it was, what mood it was. A lot of it came from the storyboard. That little misty section probably was drawn as a little storyboard or a cleanup drawing, a line that suggested that mood. Then I'm sure we must have had a different cel for that scene [with the witch]. It wouldn't be a black witch, but it might have been a dark witch and a cel on top of it. It could have been that way. In fact, I kind of remember that background getting cut in half, just before it was to be shot. By mistake somebody cut something and zip. I had put a cel over it and airbrushed it. There might have been more than one cel in that sequence, but there was a long pan.... She sits in the boat. I don't know if it's the same scene or not.

DJ: It is the same scene.

CC: Something had happened to the thing and someone had cut something with that without knowing. I think I had to add a cel to it and airbrush it, because it was about ready to be shot.

DJ: You didn't have time to repaint it. When you say you added something on a cel, what do you mean?

CC: I had probably taken another long cel and just put it on the pegs, then airbrushed it so I didn't see that cut. I just have a vague memory of it. It seemed to me it was in a spot that needed to have airbrush on it. It could have been glass. It was probably glass.

DJ: Would you have done that?

CC: It could have been on celluloid. Sometimes I think we would paint right on celluloid. It was called ox gall and it smelled awful. We could mix it with our poster paint and it would stick to the cel. It was awful-smelling stuff. But it somehow made it stick.

DJ: You do recall actually painting on glass for some of the scenes?

CC: I never did a lot of that. There were two or three other painters. Dick Anthony probably got credit on it, who I know was on *Lady and the Tramp* [much later] and probably on *Pinocchio*. He was a regular oil painter and they gave him an awful lot of *Pinocchio*: roof tops, etc. Stark Davis did a lot of the tree things in the forest, the eyes and things.

DJ: What amazes me is that they get the texture of the cement, and they did that a lot in the movie.

CC: There's one of the inside of the dwarfs' house there: Sam had that way of painting all that with grey first, and then run another wash on top of it. His way of doing it was kind of slow, kind of a buildup of modeling and then tone.

DJ: Could you describe in detail how that would be done?

CC: He had this Payne's grey, a tube of it, and for some reason he liked the grey more than a thin wash of black. He would get this modeling on, kind of the texture of … and then he'd put a yellow wash over it, after it was all dry, of course.

DJ: Would he use maybe a sponge or something to wipe it off?

CC: I believe he just ran a wash, and added water to it, and while it's puddling, would kind of model it up a little bit and then let it dry.

DJ: Did he have you finish any of the backgrounds he started?

CC: No. As I recall, once we got going on it, we just finished the whole thing. We had to use his technique so they would all look the same.

Interviewed in Winter 1988.

Katherine Kerwin (1912-2002)

Katherine Kerwin, born on January 11, 1912, joined Disney's ink and paint department as a painter on January 2, 1935. A few years later she became a "checker," a job she held until her retirement in 1977. She passed away on June 25, 2002.

Katherine Kerwin: I was born in Manchester, New Hampshire, in 1912. I always wanted to work [at Disney], when I was in high school. It was during the Depression and I kept taking my little samples over after I graduated from high school.

David Johnson: How did you come to California?

KK: In 1920 my dad had passed away, and there were four of us kids. My mother brought all four of us out here.

DJ: You were eight years old then.

KK: Yes, I was eight years old when we came out. My dad had passed away and my mother got TB from him. The doctor gave her six months to live. That's why she brought us out here. We didn't have any friends or anything out here, at first. But then we soon got them and....

DJ: Did your mother live?

KK: Yes, to eighty-three. She told the doctor, "You don't know who you're telling *that* to!" She did all the things she should and came out here and she was in the best of health. Then it was in December 1934 that they finally called me to come over and try out for working [at Disney] in Inking and Painting. [Hazel Sewell was the head of the department.] At the time, in December, I was working at Robinson's gift wrapping. There was a Depression on and you needed every dime you could get. Anyway they called me to come over there and try out. I'd work all day and then I'd take the streetcar and the bus and get out there at night and ink and paint and everything. I think they tried out a hundred people that time, many more later, but....

DJ: And this was only at night?

KK: Yes.

DJ: And you were not paid for this?

KK: Oh no, we were just trying to show what we could do.

DJ: How long was this period?

KK: It was just a couple of weeks that we did it. I think it only included about four nights in all, like Tuesday and Thursday.

DJ: Who was your teacher?

KK: Hazel Sewell.

DJ: She personally showed you?

KK: She came around and checked everything out. The first night I had beginner's luck and did real well. Then I didn't do so well, in inking. I didn't do so well the next night, because she picked up my cel and saw my name and said, "Are you Katherine Kerwin?" The next time I found paint on the table and I was painting, not inking. Of the people they tried out they had three inkers that they chose and eight painters and I was a painter.

DJ: Did you study art in high school?

KK: Just high school. I really didn't have any real good artistic background, except that I wanted to do it. And I did it at home all by myself, trying to copy the style of others. But as it turned out, I didn't have to do any original work after I got there, because I just did painting and then I ended up in final checking. The girl that did that worked opposite Hazel at her desk in a little office in the small building they had on Hyperion.

DJ: Who was that that was opposite Hazel?

KK: That was Dot Smith. She was the only final checker. We always worked Saturdays until noon at that time. She would be busy and I'd sit just outside her door and she'd come out and ask me if I wanted to help her Saturday afternoon. I'd help her all Saturday afternoon. Of course you weren't paid for all of this. We did it because we wanted to.

DJ: Were these cartoon shorts you're talking about? Because this must have been before *Snow White*.

KK: It was before. Because we were building up to *Snow White*. Then I worked with Dottie and then when there was an opening for someone to be with her, and she let me be her helper. After she became in charge of the whole ink and paint department, after they built the new building, then we went into larger quarters and she became, after Hazel left…. There was another girl that preceded her and then she was in charge of Ink and Paint and I was in charge of final checking from then on. Then, during the war years, because our work was so closely connected with the final shooting, there were about three or four of us that went out and did shooting on the camera. Just during the war years. I returned to that because so many of the fellows had to go to the war. Some of them went back to Washington D.C. and did the same work back there. That's how I got there. I wanted to work there so bad I could taste it and I just loved it. I stayed there until I was 65 and enjoyed every minute of it.

DJ: Tell me about what you remember from *Snow White*.

KK: This Evelyn Sherwood whose name I gave you, she and I had learned how to do final checking and so Dottie let Evelyn and me work all night long. They needed our space and we knew how to do it. We had a whole lot of scenes ready in the morning to go out to camera.

DJ: What exactly is a checker?

KK: It's just you check everything. You see if there's any color jump, because they usually hand out the cels in groups of twelve or so. If it's an easy set it might have more, or a hard set it might have fewer than that. But anyway they hand them out to be painted out in groups like that. They ink it on the top and turn it over and paint it on the back. Then when they pick up these sets, we get the whole scene together and we check it for one thing, for color. There might be a color jump from one set to another.

DJ: You mean they might accidentally put the wrong color on the dress or the hand?

KK: That doesn't happen often, but that's what we would check for. Then if there was any jump in the animation, we matched the pegs and put the cels so that we catch anything like that, and then we worked them mechanically. We put them on the board and make all the moves that they make in camera and if it should have been a sliding cel and wasn't, it would have to be redone. Like I say, there aren't too many mistakes that develop, but you're there to check them so in camera they don't have them. If it's a retake, we should have caught it for any reason that wasn't done by the camera department, something like that.

DJ: How do they keep the cels from getting scratchy, since they were put on top of each other?

KK: They're brand new to begin with, and then everyone has to be very careful so they don't get scratched. After they paint them, they'd come in to us and we'd check them. Then we would clean the cels and make sure there were no scratches on them.

DJ: How could you clean them without disturbing the ink and paint?

KK: You just clean around the edges of the paint. If you'd see a little smudge of paint or if there is a scratch, why, we could rub the scratch out of it.

DJ: Would you just use alcohol to clean up fingerprints?

KK: Yes, but mostly we could just do it with a soft cloth. It was a very soft cloth so that you didn't get any scratches on them.

DJ: You were wearing gloves, I assume?

KK: Not always. We were just careful. Then, if anything happened out in the camera, they'd bring a cel and we'd repair it for them. During *Snow White*, when Evelyn Sherwood and I worked all night long, then when we were finished ... we finished out of Ink and Paint on Thanksgiving Day. And that day the checking department had worked all day, and as they finished scenes they'd go home, then all night and then the next morning, keep on working all day and it was down to Dot Smith and me for the rest of the day, because we were on the last scene. And a fellow named Willoughby Hays, who passed away early but who was very liked around there, was helping us check them. And, gosh, [it was] about mid-afternoon when we finally left on Thanksgiving Day. I didn't have a car at the time and Willoughby drove me home. I sat down at the Thanksgiving dinner and fell asleep before I finished eating. But anyway it was fun to have done it all. ... You talked to Dottie on the phone?

DJ: Yes, she was apparently responsible for the color design of the dwarfs, because when she came she remembered that all the dwarfs were more or less pink and she felt that they needed to be darker, because they would be out in the woods and eating berries and things. So she thought of more burgundy and mulberry colors. She wanted a purple tunic for Grumpy. But Hazel Sewell felt that, because Walt didn't like purple.... She made up as an alternative a green overlay instead of the purple one. But they liked the purple one anyway. So even though Walt didn't like purple, they felt that purple was a better color for Grumpy. Because she thought it was a strong, sort of a grumpy color, and that's why she wanted. That's one thing she told me. I asked her about why Snow White had a yellow dress and she couldn't tell me, because she went away for two weeks on a vacation when they were deciding the color on Snow White. Do you remember anything about why they had a yellow dress?

KK: I don't remember why, but I do know that after they would have the backgrounds, they had a color model department that would make several tests of cels that would read. First of all, it had to read well against the background, and if it didn't read well, they wouldn't use a color that didn't blend with it. They would get together with the background people and they would make the final selection after the color model department would make several attempts, different colors that they would select.

When we were working on *Snow White*, Evie Sherwood and I would work all night long and then leave in the morning so they could use our space. They had so many people working. Then, when it was all out in Camera, then she and I—we got paid for this—we came and brought a good book and went in our great big rest room in our new department and we'd read and talk and sleep, and the camera guys would come in and give us a shake if we were asleep and a cel needed to be repaired.

They had a little group in Ink and Paint that would do the special things like they'd just do [special effects] to the cels, or sometimes it was done by the background people. It depends on how they were handling the picture at the time.

Boy, I tell you, Walt didn't care what it cost. Just have it very accurate. After he died, what a difference around there: "Oh, don't do it so fancy. Let it be cheaper." It took on a whole different scope after he passed away.

DJ: Did the ink-and-paint girls ever come in to look at the test animation?

KK: Yes, every time before we would start doing it in Ink and Paint, they'd run the rough stuff and let us see it, before we would work on it. Then we'd go after every daily ... the final checkers would go over with them to look at the dailies to be sure they looked good. Otherwise, they'd have a retake.

DJ: That would be the color dailies?

KK: The color dailies. But we always saw the rough reels before we started working on it.

DJ: What was the purpose of that?

KK: Just to see what we were going to be doing, to get us familiar with it all.

DJ: Do you remember your reaction seeing some of the animation for the first time, something as revolutionary as *Snow White*?

KK: Oh, gosh. We were all thrilled to death. We just liked the whole thing. We were just real thrilled about the whole thing....

The [nitrate cels] would form a gas and they'd deteriorate. I had a chest where I had tons of work with *Snow White* and had the lid down on it, and when I opened it, it was all disintegrated. It had a horrible smell from the gas that forms on the cels. It didn't take long to do that.

They kept improving the quality of paint. They'd work and work on it and put certain things in it that would make it [better]. And then they had not to put too much in or it would be sticky.

They had different things they'd stir into it to make it a little stickier but not [too] sticky. Because if they didn't put some of that in, why, it would chip and peel off and then they had problems. So they had all kinds of things like that they had to do with the paint.

DJ: How would you check camera angles, etc.?

KK: We had a camera board: the equipment that they have out in Camera, without a camera overhead. We'd make all the moves and we'd check our fields and then sometimes they'd say that we were trucking from this field to another one but by *way of* and they may ... like they'd truck from this field down to one, maybe it would be by way of this. And just once in a while we'd find an error there. They'd truck from one to the other without going by way of, and we'd have to have the background extended and things like that. We just had to check for all the mechanics of it as well as the color.

DJ: Were any of the women ever involved in story meetings?

KK: Yes, sometimes. I remember when I first worked there. You made like $18 a week in those days. And I would do a lot of gag work for the comic strips and even for the shorts. Why, they'd have meetings and run through the story and show you all the things, and they'd want gags for it. Then they'd submit gags, and I'd make sometimes more money in a month for the gags than I did from my salary ... like gags for the comic strips, for the daily strip, it would be $5 and the Sunday strip would be $10. You did those at home, at night, because you didn't have time at work. [You'd] just write them down, [not draw them].

[The queen going down the stairs was the last scene that I did] out of the checking department to the camera [department] in *Snow White*.

DJ: And you said it was difficult?

KK: It was a difficult scene. That's why it had taken so long to do, and to get through all the departments.

DJ: Why was it so difficult?

KK: It just had more mechanics and things in it. It was just a hard scene. After all these years it's hard for me to remember too much about it, except that that was the last scene that went through Ink and Paint to the camera department on *Snow White*. We sent it out on Thanksgiving Day.

Interviewed in Winter 1990.

Ink and Paint

Helen Nerbovig McIntosh (1915–1992)

In an in-depth biographical profile written for the August 1997 issue of *Animation* magazine, historian Ron Barbagallo wrote:

> An influential yet often overlooked part of the history of animation art collecting involves the inventive contributions of Disney cel inker-and-painter Helen Nerbovig. It was Helen's clever use of discarded production cel paintings and her airbrush backgrounds that came to be known throughout the animation art world as Courvoisier cel setups and Courvoisier backgrounds.

> The youngest of three daughters, Helen Gertrude Nebovig was born on August 21, 1915, in a hospital owned by her maternal grandfather located in pastoral Sheldon, Iowa. Hel's father, Halvor, a man of Norwegian descent, worked as a jeweler and watchmaker and traveled extensively for business. He moved his family to Minneapolis when Helen was approximately three years old. Helen's mother, Georgiana, surprised her husband on one of his business trips to Los Angeles and on a flip of a coin made the decision to relocate the family to the warmer climates of California.

> The Nerbovigs drove cross-country in 1924 and eventually settled in Los Angeles where Helen and her older sister Buf E. entered the local school system. In the era of Art Deco and Art Nouveau, the Nerbovig sisters studied drawing and composition one summer at the Otis Art Institute located on the edge of Mac Arthur Park. Helen's artistic abilities were already evident when, as a senior in high school, she entered a citywide poster competition and won. Her artwork was published that following year on the poster and program cover for the 1935 Easter Sunrise Service at the Hollywood Bowl. Helen graduated Hollywood High School in June 1934.

> During the Great Depression, Helen worked at a variety of art-related jobs which included packaging lipsticks for a cosmetician. She was quick to fill out an application when she heard the nearby Disney

Studio was training girls to "ink and paint" on their first feature, *Snow White and the Seven Dwarfs*. However, since the [...] training period offered at Disney was without compensation, Helen, whose family relied on her salary, sent her sister Buf to train instead. Later, Helen worked out an arrangement where she trained at Disney at night. The need for inkers and painters became so great that the Disney Studio started to pay trainees a salary of a dollar a day. With this, Helen was able to leave her day job and become one of the first paid Disney trainees.

[...] She was hired full time on May 2, 1938. Helen skillfully fit into the ink and paint department earning a starting salary of $16 a week painting cels for short subjects and features. As a hobby she assembled greeting cards for friends by taking cels left after production and assembling them against backgrounds she created using airbrush and decorative papers. It was not long before one of Helen's cel setups caught the eye of Walt Disney. [...]

Helen's cel setups so impressed Walt that he later had her prepare similar setups as VIP gifts from the Disney Studio. When San Francisco art dealer Guthrie Sayle Courvoisier formally approached the Disney brothers in the summer of 1938, Walt did not have to look far to think of someone to run a new department devoted to the design, preparation, and assembly of Disney production art for Courvoisier to distribute.

In addition to running the newly created department, around the same time, Helen also helped paint many of the three dimensional models sculpted by some of the artists from Joe Grant's character model department.

Barbagallo continued:

In the spring of 1940, Helen met her prince in the form of oil painter Robert McIntosh. Although he had been working for nearly a year in the Disney multiplane department under Dick Anthony, the couple first met while attending the ballet at the old Philharmonic Building and began their 52-year marriage on July 15, 1940. [...]

Helen also worked as a checker on Disney's 1943 feature film *Victory Through Air Power*. Later, in the publicity department [...] Helen inked and painted pages drawn by Hank Porter which appeared in *Good Housekeeping* magazine and painted the finished cover art for Deems Taylor's book on *Fantasia*. Whenever needed, Helen still created cel setups for Walt until resigning from the company on October 28, 1949, to work at home inking comic art and to be with her children.

Helen Nerbovig McIntosh died at age 76 on April 11, 1992.

[We used different pen points. A favorite was No.] 290, which is a very flexible point pen [made out of metal but not a crow quill pen]. You can never do any inking with a crow quill. [But the 290 was the very fine, very flexible pen that was used on *Snow White*].

[For storing the pens,] you have like a half-round of wood, and they drilled little holes out of it. Then they had like small, cold-cream jars that they put [a] little hole [in for] every color that you were using, and you have a pen in each one, so you never changed your pen in between inks. You have a pen in each color. They're water soluble, but, like your India inks, they would dry hard and then you could scrape back if you happened to break your line, and pick it up.

Then we had a little ebony pointer that we used, and [we] kept those sharp to make those lines absolutely perfect. You have to keep stirring [the paint]. When you'd go to lunch, you'd put a little water on them and then you'd have to cover them, wipe your pens off, because the ink would attack the pen point, too, and take the ends off your pens at times, and then you'd have to change all your points. ... Just water [to clean the pens].

You never did one cel at a time. You'd do scenes. You'd have these shelves in front of you and you always worked with a slipped cel underneath or a paper to keep them from scratching as you put them on your shelves and back. They'd just give us a stack of drawings and then they'd put them under the cels.

[You'd paint] each color. If it's all black you would ink your whole cel, but if you're working with color you'd put one color on at a time and you'd put it on your shelf. And you'd do your whole pack. If you've got twelve, fifteen, or twenty, they'd go on your shelves and you'd put them in sequence, and then you'd pull them all down as they were dry. At the end of your thing they were pretty dry, and you'd stack them all up and take your next color and go again.

And they'd have somebody that would do a cel and they'd time it and if you wanted to work you made your time. You didn't play around for two minutes. We had one break in the morning and one in the afternoon.

You had to have such control that it's fantastic. I look at it today and I marvel that we ever did that. (I lost my sight at one point. My sister had to take me home. I couldn't see the clock at the end of the corridor.) You work off the end of your elbow and you make a long swing. You don't do finger work. You can't use your fingers at all. [Even very small details like eyes and mouth], you still work from your elbow.

And then the lifting of you pen to taper your lines ... or if you're going to do a heavier line you put your pen down a little heavier and then you lift and you got to do all of that from your elbow. It's more like Oriental brush work. So that's the difference between ink and paint: the perfection of the line you had to reach and keep.

Interviewed in Winter 1990.

Grace Godino (1915–2011)

Grace Godino spent her whole career at the Disney Studio as a talented painter. She was born on September 27, 1915, got an art major from Santa Monica City College in 1932, and was hired by Disney on May 10, 1937. By April 5, 1965, the last date to be mentioned on her company profile, she was still working in Ink and Paint for the studio.

Historian Harvey Deneroff wrote on Cartoon Research:

> Godino had been an art major in college before she was hired, initially inking and then also painting, and working in the shadow department with Wilma Baker on special-effects animation. Most of her animation career was at Disney, but she did brief stints elsewhere, working for Walter Lantz, Hanna-Barbera, Ron Campbell Films, Marvel, and UPA, as well as being a color modeler on the very un-Disney *The Nine Lives of Fritz the Cat*.

> Like some other inkers and painters, she had interests outside of animation. For instance, she had something of an acting career and worked with future movie star Glenn Ford at a production at Miles Playhouse, in Santa Monica, during the 1930s; her friendship with Ford led her to become a stand-in for superstar Rita Hayworth in her most iconic film, *Gilda* (1946), as well as *The Loves of Carmen* (1948). She did some voiceover work and was a model for the character of Madame Adelaide Bonfamille in *The Aristocats*. After retiring from animation, she became a watercolorist and had her own studio, called appropriately enough The Mouse Trap.

Grace Godino: [We got a small remuneration] for gas. I think it was like $10 a week to just train [my training period was three months]. And they dropped like flies. You'd have little pink slips: you'd be working at your desk and these little pink slips would come along and you'd sit there trembling and "am I going to be the one that's thrown out?" because you wanted to be there so badly. I survived that and then the work job. Then you got $16 a week. That was a big thing.

It was good training. It worked. You stayed right with it to try to learn your craft. You worked in practically every department, except Animation. Walt didn't want women animators and he had good reason. Women get married and have children and he didn't want the interruptions. He wanted to hold on [to] those men.

[Being at Disney's] was so fascinating to me and we were *so* gung-ho. I remember the first time we went, when the picture was not completed but it was in storyboard form, and some of it was animated but it was just the drawings and then a few scenes in color that we had done.

And we were all invited on the soundstage and we all sat on the floor. [It was a] small soundstage. We saw the full picture for the first time. *I never had such a thrill in my life!* In fact, it chokes me up right now because as we sat there we realized what it was: it was so new and so beautiful. And the songs! They had all [the] music. It had some orchestration and some they filled in, and Walt was there and they would talk. Somebody'd get up and narrate a little section that wasn't quite finished and explain things and we walked out of there and were like ten feet tall. And you started singing the songs: they were so strong, so great. We came back through the corridor singing "Whistle While You Work" and all these things. I preferred *that* to any picture of *Snow White* I saw since then. When I saw the opening it was a thrill, too, but the big thrill was to see it in the rough!

Interviewed on February 4, 1990.

Virginia "Geno" Pearson

Geno Pearson served as an inker at the Disney Studio during the making of *Snow White and the Seven Dwarfs*. We could not locate additional information about her life and career.

Geno Pearson: [I submitted a portfolio] and they called me, out of a hundred girls which they accepted. There were many more than that [who] applied. But they took a hundred of us and they put us in one of the wings, all by ourselves, and we had to do inking on cels. We'd all been artists, but that's a special deal. Out of one hundred there were eight of us left. And we didn't get a cent for it.

I was living at the Hollywood Studio Club for Girls, and it cost me seven and a half [dollars a week]. Two meals a day and room. I had to go by streetcar and transfer at Beverly [Drive] to go out to Hyperion. That was five cents a day. So my dad had to help me a little bit. And if we could get out to have a dinner date, why, they'd take thirty-five cents off the evening meal price.

I think it was eight weeks we went to school without anything and then we were laid off. I went back pretty soon, maybe two or three weeks later. Then they called us up and we went to work at $8 [a week] for half a day, six days a week. I worked for about three weeks and they put me on full time at $16.

Interviewed on March 6, 1990.

Erna Englander (1909-2008)

Erna Englander was the wife of Disney storyman Otto Englander.

David Johnson: [Could you tell me about] life at the studio at that time and what were your impressions about Walt.

Erna Englander: I tell you, it was the most exciting, intoxicating time for all the artists, because that was the first [feature-length animated movie]. Everybody had so much enthusiasm. They worked overtime, without pay ... that goes without saying. They were so excited that.... That was way before drugs or everything else and they were all high, absolutely. They were walking on air. They realized that with this *Snow White* feature Disney was taking them into another dimension. He had opened all possibilities because when it comes to imagination, there is no limitation where the mind can take you and your creativity. After that, they got excited and everything else, but it was not like this. It was absolutely euphoric. That would be the thing. And every time they could hardly wait for something, any sequence to be filmed, so they could watch it. And they really worked hard. But they were never happier, I will tell you that. Never!

DJ: Even Otto wasn't happy [afterward]?

EE: They were happy, but I cannot.... This is impossible to describe. It was, as I said, euphoria. I think they were euphoric. They were carried on this enthusiasm, all of them, from the secretaries up to Disney. Everybody was excited. Everybody, including the wives. Because whenever there was a sequence, we would always say, "Can we come and see? Can we come and see?"

DJ: Did you go?

EE: Of course. The studio was only a few minutes from here.

DJ: Do you remember the first time that you saw anything to do with *Snow White*?

EE: Yes. I remember very well. It was Marjorie Belcher's thing and they were testing her to see how she would work. The prince they were not very happy with. He was a little stilted, a little stiff. But he didn't have much to do. That was the first that I saw.

DJ: Had they already filmed her or were they actually filming her when you went?

EE: They filmed her and they were also showing the animation from that.

DJ: You didn't keep a diary, did you?

EE: No! I had my own business. I was a foreign correspondent. I had my work, [Otto] had his work.

DJ: How often would you go to see the work as it progressed along?

EE: Whenever there was something to be seen, my husband would call and say, "Come on, five o'clock we're showing...." And we'd all be there. Here would be ten of us after that going to dinner in twenty cars. It was a very exciting time, I can tell you that.

DJ: Now Otto, after he got on *Snow White*, did he work on it almost every day?

EE: Of course, from nine till sometimes midnight.

DJ: Did he take the work home here?

EE: Never. But they worked hard. Nobody watched the clock. What carried them was not the pay, not any of that thing. Because at that time they didn't have the unions. They didn't get all that, except the executives had good salaries. But I can't complain either. What carried them was this tremendous enthusiasm. They were all aware that they were doing something that had never been done before. I was very fortunate. I had an assignment in France. And I went there to the opening of *Snow White* in Paris.

DJ: How did the French take it?

EE: They went wild! ... The premiere here was by invitation only. Not just Disney people but all the important people, the movie stars. I will never forget [it]. My husband and I, Ted Sears and his wife, were walking together. We came together. People on the sidelines [were waiting to see] a group of stars. And somebody said, "Who's that?" And the one in front said, "That's nobody!" [Laughs] We were hysterical. We told Disney about it. They were expecting movie stars, but we were nobody as far as they're concerned. Ted Sears said, "I should have turned around and said, 'Without him and me, YOU wouldn't be here! *Snow White* wouldn't be there!" But of course he didn't say it.

Everything had to be just perfect. It was unbelievable. When I think back so many years, I can see their faces: they were absolutely transformed, transfigured, euphoric. All of them. There was not *one* that did not share this.

DJ: Except Art Babbitt! [Laughs] He was a very unpleasant personality.

EE: Very! He was married to Marge.

DJ: But only for a year.

EE: He was such a homely son-of-a-gun.

[...]

I was picketing [during the strike].

DJ: You were !?

EE: Yeah. Most of the wives. We were picketing while our husbands were working in there. They were executives. So Otto was not on strike. That was really quite something. He would come home and I wouldn't talk to him.

DJ: Because you believed they should strike?

EE: Yeah. I believed in unions.

DJ: But yet you admired Walt at the same time.

EE: [That] had nothing to do with it. I admired him, but I felt that the inkers and painters are losing their eyes. They're getting $30 a week. Let's face it. They were being....

DJ: Exploited.

EE: I'm a Yugoslav. All Yugoslavs are fighters. You know, we fought four German divisions during the Second World War. That's what made possible El Alamein, our victory and everything else. Anyway.

I remember when Babbitt was arrested. We were all there picketing. Most of the wives of these guys who worked … that was during the *Dumbo* thing. But they won and then Disney had to take everybody back, including Babbitt.

DJ: Well, did you ever have a conversation with him personally?

EE: You mean Walt Disney?

DJ: Yes.

EE: Oh, yes! Because I interviewed him for the newspapers that I was writing for.

DJ: You did?

EE: Yes.

DJ: What was your impression of the man?

EE: I tell you: the man was a visionary. I will tell you a little incident. He would sit in this Coral Room for executives' luncheon. It was a special room. And we belonged there. I could come and bring guests. Disney would sit with Otto, with Ted Sears, with Les Clark, and whoever he would be sitting with at the table. He would get up and he would come to our table and be as charming and effusive and as polite as he could be. And we would wave back at him. He would go back and would tell, "You see, you little bastards, you're going to go home tonight, and you're going to tell your wives what a son-of-a-bitch Disney is. They won't believe you, I just charmed them!" That's the kind a guy he was. There was also something very nasty you probably might hear: that he was anti-Semitic. That's not true. [Note: Erna Englander was herself Jewish.]

He used to say when he would get mad, he would tell the guys, the story department I'm talking about, he'd say, "OK you eggheads, you all have college degrees, you all have this and that. I only have high school but you're working for me!" That was the meanest thing when he would get mad, he would tell them, when he didn't like a storyline or whatever. "You smart college boy."

DJ: "Smart asses" he would say.

EE: Exactly. Not only that. He said "I will chew your ass, if that isn't ready by tomorrow!" He would say that, yes, he did. He was very vulgar.

DJ: He came from the farm, you know.

EE: My husband would defend him. He'd say, "He's very earthy, honey. You're just European. You're just too formal." He's earthy. So what! That's the way he talked. I said, "Good, that's nice."

DJ: What do you think made him unique? Obviously, he was a unique person.

EE: He certainly was.

DJ: In a way he was kind of a genius about certain things, but he wasn't a genius like some people are. Like you would say Stravinsky or someone like that.

EE: I will tell you very frankly, and I will tell it to you in his own words. Maybe he would be criticized in the papers about some film or Silly Symphony or something. He would say, "I don't care. I'm not making films for the guys who read *The New Yorker*, like you. I'm making it for America. He had a feeling, he had an unerring feeling what will go, what will not go, and most of the time he was right. You see, he was one of them.

DJ: He was one of the people, you mean.

EE: Exactly. And he had his finger on it. But he was a great visionary. I will never forget when he took us someplace way out of nowhere, in Valencia, and we stood up on a hill—just a few of his favorite "white-haired boys." My husband would say, "I'm losing all my hair and he's still calling me a 'white-haired boy!'" We would go there and he would tell us how it's going to be built, this CalArts [school], where they would teach: animation, where they would do this. And he would just go into ecstasy. We looked around. I saw nothing but fields. I mean the man was incredibly visionary. And sure enough, where we were standing is a fantastic school. It's a fantastic thing and I will never forget that and I said to my husband, "You know, I'm sure he's going to do it." Because he does everything [he says he's going to]. He could see it. It's a pity. He killed himself with the smoking. Three, four packs a day.

DJ: I know. Well, I think he was a driven man.

EE: He was.

DJ: He was really a country bumpkin at heart.

EE: He was a hick, we know that. Otto had that letter from him to the counsel and from different senators and everything, to speed up my visa. When he first met me, when I came, I didn't speak English. Fortunately, for him! I didn't know what he said then. Later on, my husband told me [that Walt had] said [about me], "You had to go for that to Yugoslavia? You could have found this here!" And he smiled. My husband was a gentleman and he didn't tell me till *years later*! I said, "You thought that I didn't speak English. *I know* what you said!" He said, "Oh, boy!" He was like that, you know Disney! He was charming. He could charm a snake.

DJ: Yes, I guess he could. That's why he always got his own way.

EE: Sure he did. Sure he did.

The night before the *Snow White* premiere, I don't think any of us slept, because we wanted to see how it's going to be received. And the people in the audience stood up and gave him a standing ovation.

[After the premiere] it was a tremendous let-down. They were all worried, knocked-up. Not the next day. My husband said, "What are we going to do for an encore that'll ever top *Snow White*?" They were all worried about it.

[...]

[Norm Ferguson:] small guy and very friendly and somehow intro-verted. He was not very outgoing. Les Clark on the contrary was all out. He's a real Irishman. [That guy] had a dog and the dog was in the apartment eight hours and he would ring his telephone and then when the telephone would ring, his dog would start going crazy run-ning. Ours did, too. And so, one day Ted Sears went to the manager and asked for a key, and she knew him because he was coming in and out. Ted knew exactly when he's going to call up to the dog and Ted Sears picks up the phone and says, "Woof, woof," and the guy almost fainted. Ted would do things like that.

[...]

[It wasn't that Walt] couldn't [give compliments]. He wouldn't. He wouldn't. He was the most unhappy man when the union won, when the strike was over. Because, you see, he was the great white father over all his children, and in a way they did look up at the father image. They tried to emulate him and they wanted him to be proud of them. They wanted to be patted on the shoulder, and he was very stingy with his praise. And Otto would tell me, many times: "I hope he doesn't say anything again like 'white-haired boy,' or 'that was terrific, Otto,' because the rest are going to hate me." There was tremendous jealousy for his attention and affection. And he was very stingy with it.

Let me tell you about the Hollywood Bowl. Disney had a box. Eight-ten. He would say, "Come on, you eggheads." He would give us [tickets] and we would invite our friends. We would go and the photographer would come, take a look at us and not take a picture because it wasn't Disney. He never went to the Hollywood Bowl. He had a number-one parking lot. We would come in there ... it was marvelous. My husband got all those tickets.

Interviewed on March 11, 1990.

Elly Horvath (1896–1996)

Elly Horvath was the wife of Disney concept artist Ferdinand Horvath.

Elly Horvath: [Walt] wanted [my husband Ferdinand] to come out. Disney said, "I'll send you the money to come out with." It was on the train, and my husband said, "It should be first class, I don't want to travel third class." We laughed that it would be first class. He also said he wanted to know how much money he would get by the week or so. Walt said, "If you are here and you are good you can make as much money as you can." And my husband said, "How much is that in dollars and cents?" I think it was $25 for a week. Anyhow, then he came out.

David Johnson: And you went with him?

EH: No, I did not.

DJ: Oh, you stayed in NY?

EH: I stayed in NY. He said, "Let's see what's going on."

DJ: Where were you living in NY?

EH: On Riverside Drive. Uptown Riverside Drive.

DJ: About 110ᵗʰ Street?

EH: Something like that. I didn't like it much. I had put on awnings on the windows in all the buildings. Then he went to the studio and he liked it and then I went out to him after a few months. I think it was a few months that the trial was going on. So after a few months I went out and the Disney Studio was on Hyperion. It was a nice studio and I was introduced to Walt and he said, "Welcome to the family. This is going to be a family." I liked it in the beginning. The first weekend he said we should all come out horseback riding here.

There were horses for us and [for] the whole studio. He wanted to have the studio and the people always together. So Sundays we went all out horseback riding.

DJ: Had you been horseback riding before that?

EH: Yes. But anyhow, those horses didn't need that kind of thing to ride on because they hardly could walk. Old horses. And once I looked over them one horse had that much open wound in there. I told Walt, "Did you see the horses?" "No." I said, "Why don't you look what they are for?" He looked at it and said, "We can change that." So he got the horse out of there. Sundays and weekdays my husband went in the mornings, and afternoons, and he went in the evenings. After a few weeks, I said to Walt, "You know I am a married woman. I like my husband home once in a while." He said, "I want him every evening. *I* come in every evening." I said, "It's your business. It's a different story. We can't do that." If there was a story conference, the girls should come in also to make coffee. So he wanted to make it so that it's a home thing.

DJ: Did you like him?

EH: Oh yeah.

DJ: What was he like?

EH: Walt had very little schooling. And I had a university degree and my husband had ... and that was something above him, you know. If ever he wanted to know he asked my husband [who] was a gentleman and a scholar.

DJ: What was your degree in?

EH: Medicine.

DJ: Oh, you were going to be a doctor, then? But you didn't continue?

EH: I didn't finish.

DJ: Because you met your husband?

EH: Yes. And he promised me a career.

DJ: In what?

EH: He said, "I give you a career for life if you marry me."

DJ: Oh, a housewife, you mean?

EH: Yeah, that's a career. Lilly [Disney, Walt's wife] asked me what kind of color my husband liked because he wanted to make the room up. My husband got the same color. Because it's always good for an artist to have the same color he likes where he has to work.

DJ: At the studio.

EH: Yes, at the studio.

DJ: Yes, I know Walt was not very sophisticated, either.

EH: He had very little schooling.

DJ: But you liked him, you enjoyed his company.

EH: Oh yes. Because, for instance, he said, "Elly, we go to a theater tonight." He took us to the theater and said, "You sit here and I here." It was a ballet. He knew I was a ballet dancer.

DJ: Oh, you were?

EH: I started out with ballet dancing, because I had very good connections. My uncle was minister of education and I could go to the theater and finish school if I was not seen in the street after six o'clock in the morning, things like this.

In the theater I had to explain to Walt, who'd ask "What does that style [mean]?" "It's a *plié*," things like this. He was very eager to know and to get educated in the things he was not, for instance, medicine. He wanted to know about why do you give some medicines for headache. How does it work? He always wanted to know something.

DJ: He was quite brilliant in his own way.

EH: Oh, yes. For instance, there was a picture made and we all have to come in to see it. It was brought out and he says, "Give me the roll [of film], I'll put it in the garbage." I said, "What's wrong?" "I don't know. It's no good." The whole thing, a week's work, and we run it, and he said, "It's no good. Put it in the garbage. The public won't like it. I can see it! It's no good." He had a special, wonderful sense to find out and to put his finger on what the public would like and do it beautifully.

DJ: And what was his wife like?

EH: She was in the background, always. A few other wives, for instance Ferguson's wife, they were together a lot. [Showing a photo.] Here's my husband with a knife. You know why?

DJ: No.

EH: Because if something was not good, he said, "I cut it out!"

DJ: What was Norman Ferguson like?

EH: Jovial.

DJ: Was he well trained in art or was he a natural?

EH: Whether he was trained or not I do not know, but he was very great.

DJ: I know he drew the Big Bad Wolf in *Three Little Pigs*.

EH: Three people say they did. A long time ago, they had some argument and they're sitting together and they said, "Wait a minute! That wasn't you." Somebody else said, "I made it." But they all worked on it. So in the end, which was the original then I don't really know.

Margie Champion was modeling for my husband, the movements.

DJ: I know that your husband did a lot of work very early on, on the dwarfs, but he wasn't given any credit.

EH: Nobody was ever given any credit. Once one of the boys, it was Babbitt, said, "If we don't get any credit, we are not going to work" So Walt said, "All right, either you get a bonus or you want to have credit." My husband wanted credit rather the bonus.

DJ: You said your husband was involved in the story conferences. But he drew a lot of the sketches. Do you remember anything in particular of his involvement on *Snow White*?

EH: I know that he was making the movements of Margie. That's why we met her. She was posing and he was making the drawings of the movements.

DJ: But in addition to that he would also be in Story.

EH: He worked on the stories. As a matter of fact, what was that mill story?

DJ: *The Old Mill*.

EH: *The Old Mill*. He made it from the beginning and I even have someplace the original model he made.

DJ: How often did you visit the studio?

EH: When there were story conferences, we all went. They all came in.

DJ: Even the wives.

EH: The wives.

DJ: You were at the premiere on *Snow White* in Los Angeles, weren't you?

EH: Yes.

DJ: Had you been seeing it in bits and pieces before then?

EH: It didn't make any impression on me. I didn't care about it much. There was so much in the beginning. They were making it. It was fine, and they looked at it and Walt didn't like it, so they made another of the same thing. Then the third time.... And I always fell asleep. They waited for what was wrong now, should they make it again.

DJ: And this was very common during the *Snow White* era?

EH: Yes.

DJ: So you just got fed up with it.

EH: To see it again and again.

DJ: Also because you weren't probably that interested in animation, maybe.

EH: Animation was really not my husband's métier, he was an artist and not a cartoonist. He did that because it came easy for him.

DJ: What about Art Babbitt. I know he didn't get along very well with Walt.

EH: Art Babbitt opened his mouth and Walt didn't like it.

DJ: But what was your impression of Art?

EH: I liked him. In the beginning I liked him. Then I didn't because he was....

DJ: He had a chip on his shoulder, I think.

EH: More than that. He was drinking. I think Margie once said that he was doping or something. But he was very smart. He was Jewish. And he was very smart and he said, "If we don't hold together...." He was the one who said put fire under all the cartoonists. He was good. He was the rebel.

DJ: But it was Walt who really had the whole vision and it was very important. And I don't think Art understood that.

EH: He did. We all appreciated it. Mostly what he said he wants to put down was done. He wanted something to be done and they did it. To an artist he could say exactly what he wanted, how he wanted it, how small, funny or something.... He could suggest that to you and the artist could understand it and work it out.

Interviewed on September 11, 1987.

Bob Cook
(1903–1995)

Soundman Bob Cook joined the Disney Studio in 1929 and retired in 1971. This interview gives us insight into the little-known world of Disney's sound experts. It also sheds new light on the early days of an obscure Disney venture, the Disney Film Recording Company.

From "Disneys Form Sound Recording Co., Independent's Business Sought," in the trade magazine *Sound Waves*, dated April 15, 1929:

> The first mobile "sound on film" equipment for independent producers' use will soon make its appearance in Hollywood. It is being built for Walter and Roy Disney, producers for many years of animated cartoons. This sound unit was designed by William Garity, the Disney chief engineer, and George Lowerre, his assistant, both DeForest experts.
>
> According to Walter Disney, the entire outfit will be mounted on two trucks, the smaller of which will be available for direct contact with studio sets. The device has as its nucleus a Powers' Cinephone, which records all sound direct on the film. A crew of pioneer sound-on-film experts will accompany the trucks. The Disney Brothers, who will operate the device as the Disney Film Recording Corporation, are at present using the basic equipment to record sound for their current short subjects.
>
> As we go to press, it is learned that this equipment is ready now. The major truck is of one and one-half ton capacity while the recording will be done on film, using the glow-lamp process instead of the light valve. The Disney Brothers plan to do no producing on their own at present, with the exception of the sound cartoons Mickey Mouse (1/2 reelers), six of which have been made already, meeting with great success.
>
> The rental prices of the trucks have not been decided on at present, but a reasonable rental can be expected. It is said that Carl Stalling, as music director for the organization, is prepared to handle the music synchronization, compositions, etc., necessary for independent units.

The rest of the story is told by Bob Cook.

David Johnson: I would like to know just a little about your background, where you're from, and how you came to the Disney Studio and what year.

Bob Cook: I'm from Wisconsin. Born on September 27, 1903. My background was in radio. I had great interest in radio. The town that I was born in had a seaport and I saw those ships coming in and out, and there was a big radio-telegraph station there to communicate with the ships. I saw that big antennae down there at the end of the street and I was always fascinated by it, by the fact that you could talk to ships without wires. So I got an amateur license in 1921—my first amateur radio license—and got out of high school and went to work for Chicago-Northwestern Railroad. I was a car clerk, they called it. Then went to radio school in Valparaiso, Indiana, where I studied to be a commercial radio operator. I got out of school and went to work on a passenger ship. Of course, on the Great Lakes, in the winter time it's all frozen up and there's no navigation, except car ferries—no passenger business. So I got on that passenger ship, which was called the *Mamitou*, and finished the first season. The ship laid up in September, getting pretty cold then and windy and not very many passengers anymore. Then I went to work for a car ferry line, which was the Ann Arbor Railroad, and hauled trade cars across Lake Michigan. They ran all year round. Those ships were built for ice-breaking and any kind of weather. About that time my parents moved to California and I came out to visit them once or twice. I also got fascinated with the Los Angeles area and wanted to get a job here if I could, but I found there was no call for radio men around this area at that time, although the broadcast business was just beginning.

DJ: What year was this?

BC: This was 1925 and I went back to my regular duties again, part time on ship.

DJ: Where was this ship? Was it out of Long Beach?

BC: No, this was back in Wisconsin.

DJ: Oh, we're still on the Great Lakes.

BC: Lake Michigan. I went back there several times and finally got into a radio telegraph shore station, the one that speaks to the ships by radio telegraph. That happened to be in my hometown, which, of course, was part of my ambition: to work in my home town in this big radio station. But my folks had moved away so I was living in a boarding house.

DJ: What did your parents do for a living?

BC: My father was the [garbled] for the Chicago-North Western Railroad, practically all his working life.

DJ: He also worked for them in Los Angeles?

BC: No, in his real early days, before he was married, he was a barber and he couldn't find any work out here. He did apply with the Southern Pacific and they said they could give him occasional work, but he had to work his way up through the seniority again. Of course, they couldn't survive on that. So he went to a school for women's hair cutting—permanent waves, all that sort of thing—here in Los Angeles. Then finally he opened a shop of his own and did quite well, too, down on Hill Street in Los Angeles. At that time there were quite a few theaters that had live talent on the stages. So he had quite a clientele of women customers that came, oh, sometimes two or three times a week, get their hair fixed, and permanent waves, and so on. They kept writing me all the time to get away from that cold weather and come out here—it's so nice. And in those days it was. No smog, and beautiful weather. I tried it several times but never could find any work.

In the meantime, working in my home town in that big radio station I had some spare-time evenings. I'd built a little broadcasting station, which, incidentally, is still in operation. This was 1925. I got the license and did the whole thing. It was located in a theater and that gave me quite a bit of experience. Building the thing helped quite a bit. I was already licensed by the Federal Communications Commission, so that was all in my favor. I came out here a second or third time, and finally did get a job in a broadcast station which was KMTR in Hollywood. The reason I got it was that in my home town my father, being a railroad man, and me, being interested in telegraphy, I used to go down to the railroad depot and learned telegraph code, which was different than radio code. Very difficult to do, and practically nobody ever did it. But I finally mastered that code, too, so I knew both codes: the one that's used by Western Union and the one that's used by radio on ships. A lot of people said, "What do you want to learn that [for]?" That was what got me the job in broadcasting in Hollywood. They were getting a telegraph line in there, and they needed licensed radio men to operate their broadcast equipment. But they also needed a man to operate the telegraph. So they had a list of applicants about two feet long, but none of them knew both codes. That's what got me the job. It came in very handy, because the broadcasting got on a network which was just forming at that time.... All the communication between the network stations was handled by telegraph through the telephone company, American Telephone and Telegraph Company. And by knowing both codes, no matter who got on the network, if you didn't know one code, he knew the other one. And I used to handle messages both ways. But the phone company, sometimes at the end of each network broadcast, asked the comments from every station that took the program. And a great many of the broadcast engineers along the route didn't know the telegraph code. I always remember that first transcontinental broadcast....

DJ: What kind of a radio station was this? What kind of programs?

BC: Oh, gosh, about everything. They were not very different from today. They had singers, they had big orchestras. Of course, that was a little different. They had big symphony orchestras in those days. Standard Oil was one of the big sponsors.

DJ: So they did classical music on your program, too?

BC: Quite a bit, yeah. And we had a pianist and a vocalist that had a very popular program: *The Happiness Hour.* I think it was KMTR. We played records, and it was a regular broadcast sponsored by the Standard Oil Company. It was a very good broadcast symphony orchestra. They started the program saying, "This program is sponsored by a Standard Oil Company in California," and that same announcement was made at the end, and that was all the commercial part of it in those days. Everybody enjoyed that, no interruptions, no hard sell or anything. Of course, we worked day and night, although in those days in the afternoon, from noon till about four o'clock they found there weren't very many listeners, so we used to shut down the transmitter and do maintenance work, or do other things. Sometimes [we'd] go home for three or four hours in the intervening time, then start it up again. We never worked past midnight. We always signed off at midnight, and then started up at five in the morning again.

I stuck with that for over a year, and the station was gradually going bankrupt. About that time we heard about sound coming into movies and finally also heard through the underground that we wouldn't be getting paid ... very soon the checks would bounce, which happened to be true. Three of us engineers looked around, and we found there was a movie studio down on Melrose Avenue. That was the closest one. That's the only reason we went there. It happened to be a little independent studio called Tech-Art and it only had two stages. Anyway, we went there and they had just got their shipment of RCA sound recording equipment and they hired all three of us at one time. This was a rental lot, and Roy Disney had an idea to go into the recording business while his brother Walt was in the cartoon business. So Roy Disney rented a little stage, not much bigger than this living room, actually, on this Tech-Art lot. While we didn't work for him at that time, we saw him a lot, and then, once in a while, his brother Walt would come over and we finally got acquainted, and that's how I met Walt Disney. That's also how I met Roy Disney, his older brother. I finally got to know them better and better through daily contact. We were usually working seven days a week. And one day Walt said, "If you have a little time, come in here and see if this is funny. We've just finished a cartoon." We had a little time and we went in and....

DJ: Where was that Disney studio?

BC: 2719 Hyperion. He was established there, and Roy Disney was established over on Melrose Avenue. When we weren't busy recording we would come over to Hyperion and do electrical work or anything that they needed. Everything was non-union then for us, so it kept us busy, and we often spent time at the cartoon studio and gradually got acquainted with people there, too.

DJ: You liked Walt? You thought he was a nice guy?

BC: At that time, of course, we were very impressed with him, especially with his imagination and his sense of humor, and his cartoons were very funny. I always remember *Skeleton Dance* with the fellow playing the xylophone on the ribs. So we were pretty flattered to even know him. Everybody was, because he had such an imagination and so much drive. While we were there, all at once, just almost overnight, there was a demand for sound recording and everybody that had a little money immediately wanted to make a picture with sound, because the theaters were begging for sound movies. So Roy hired a salesman and got some business too. But the trouble was a lot of the business people didn't have the money to pay for the sound, and when the picture was finished they were in debt so deeply that we didn't get our pay.

We finally found one or two good customers. One of them was Mascot Pictures, who made serials. And we shot twenty-nine consecutive days when they photographed these things, mostly westerns. John Wayne was one of our early actors in the serial. In fact, I think it was on the third or fourth picture he ever made that I worked with him. We called him Duke in those days. His name was really Duke Morrison [Note: Actually, it was Marion Mitchell Morrison]. He had been a prop man and he was quite a ham actor. But he had a good voice, and he had what it took, no doubt about that. He had a talent that just needed some polishing up and that came later, when he made.

We made another picture which I enjoyed a lot, having quite a railroad background by that time. It was called *The Hurricane Express*. That was for Mascot Pictures, too. That wasn't so terribly difficult. But [for] the westerns we used to go to Kernville, California, in very mountainous country.

DJ: Why wouldn't they go around here?

BC: There're several reasons. One was that there are some big ranches around there, so they had plenty of horses and cowboys. Another one was the very scenic country. There was the Kern River, which we used a lot, too, and mountains, meadows, branches, all that sort of thing. No power poles or telephone poles or towers or anything like that in the picture. It'd be very different today, of course. The Kern River was a real rushing, beautiful river in those days. It went down through Kern Canyon, which was quite a canyon, too. Very scenic country. It was spotted with old gold mines, so they used the old gold mines and the outer water wheels. We also shot some of those serials up in Victorville and one of the reasons was there was a band of wild horses up around there at that time. The cowboys rounded them all up and used them in the picture and then sold them to a dog food company. That was an interesting picture, too, and I remember we did that in the fall of the year, in the daytime. In the afternoons it got so hot everybody stripped down to their waist, and at night there was ice in the water troughs. There was a big difference in temperature.

Every one of those serials were made [over] twenty-nine consecutive days. It didn't matter if there was a holiday or anything else in there. We worked from the time the sun came up till after the sun went down, usually with a few lights. And if you could stand that you could stand almost anything. It was really rugged going. In those mountains in Kernville, of course, we had to pull all those cables around and camera movers.

And then we did the sound for some regular movies, too, which kept us busy often times seven days a week and often times from eight in the morning until midnight. One picture we made, we worked for three companies the same day, and worked through the night and didn't get any sleep till the following night. We worked all day on Columbia Ranch with Buck Jones, who was a famous cowboy actor. Then in the evening there was a movie called *Star of Hollywood* [probably *Playthings of Hollywood*]. And then at midnight we started out over in Hollywood and shot another picture till six in the morning. The company just gave us box lunches, and that's all. We survived, as far as food went, and the salary was a flat $65 a week, regardless of any hours we worked. So it wasn't very rewarding as far as money went. Pretty rugged life. My wife thought I was insane to work those kinds of hours and I didn't see much of her, either.

DJ: Now was this before the Depression started, in the late twenties, or are you talking about the early thirties now?

BC: Both.

DJ: Because $65 was a lot of money during the Depression. Some of the animators were only getting $16 a week when they started in 1935.

BC: It was pretty good, except that, again, the Tech-Art checks bounced, and I had a whole handful of them and nobody would cash them. Sixty-five dollars would have been a pretty good salary in those days, that's right. You weren't getting much by the hour. You earned every cent.

DJ: So you were already married at this time.

BC: Yeah, I got married when I was working at KMTR, in the broadcast station, in 1928.

DJ: Was your wife from this area?

BC: No. I went back to Wisconsin and got married. I knew her back there. Of course, when the Depression hit.... I never will forget that, because we had just gone to a furniture company downtown, Barker Brothers, and bought all our furniture, and then about two or three days after we signed up for the furniture with monthly payments, the Depression hit, practically overnight. That was 1929. We really did some scraping. We tried to keep up the payments and then one time we had about forty dollars left, and that was it. We were renting a little bungalow over in Hollywood. It was a rough go, but somehow we got through it. Especially working for Disney's, the checks never bounced.

DJ: How did you finally get started to work [for Disney] more permanently?

BC: Tech-Art Studios started to go bankrupt and we had a handful of checks that we couldn't cash, each one of us. One day Roy Disney said, "This place is about to fold up. How would you like to work for us?" We said, "Oh, well, sure!" So that's how we went to work for Roy Disney. And working for him we did these serials, but also when Walt wanted to record we did his recording for the cartoons. So it was kind of a dual thing for a while.

DJ: What was Roy Disney working on then?

BC: He had a little office there and it was his sound company.

DJ: When did he dissolve that and just go entirely with his brother?

BC: That was in 1930. Outside of one or two good customers, we had a lot of work but no money coming in. And one day Roy Disney said, "You know, this place is about to fold up. How would you like to work for us?" So...that's how we went to work for Roy Disney and [later] we moved over to Hyperion and they built a soundstage over there.

DJ: That was when you were working there that they built the soundstage or had they already built it before you came?

BC: No, they built it when I was working for them.

DJ: Did you help them design it?

BC: A little bit, not too much. I remember one thing: the electrical part of it. In those days we had several floods, and I insisted that we have some lights. The sound stage didn't have a window in the whole thing. It was a fairly good-sized stage. Several times.... In 1938, we had a big flood and the soundstage flooded and there wasn't an emergency exit light in the place and a couple of fellows got caught in there and couldn't find their way out. So I did a few things, but I didn't help in the preliminary design.

DJ: You said you insisted on the electrical....

BC: The emergency lights.

DJ: Was the soundstage built in 1930 the same one used *Snow White*?

BC: Yes.

DJ: How big was it?

BC: It was fairly good sized. I would say, in those days anyway, they considered it fairly good sized. It was probably sixty or seventy feet wide and maybe a hundred-and-twenty-five feet long, something like that. [The Hyperion sound stage was undoubtedly smaller than the dimensions Bob gave. Perhaps he was confusing it with the one at the Burbank studio.]

DJ: Did it have seats like a theater or was it completely open?

BC: It was mainly a shooting stage, but it had some seats, too, for the people that were supervising: they could sit there and kind of watch the artist and make comments. Mainly it was a big, empty stage with no supports anywhere, except the walls: a big cavern, really. Sound wise, acoustically, it was a good stage, it worked very well.

About that time, the Depression was going full blast and I got an awful scare, because Roy Disney called me and said, "You know, Walt doesn't have very much sound work anymore. We think we will eventually, but right now we're kind of low on money so I think I'll have to lay you off." Of course, my heart hit the floor and then bounced back up again because there was no work whatever in those days. He said, "I'm giving you two weeks' notice." Of course I applied everywhere I could but couldn't find any work. Then I get a call from Roy Disney and he said, "How would you like to try film editing?" Of course, that was just coming in at that time: all the work on *Snow White* was coming in to be edited and assembled and everything.

DJ: What happened in the meantime, between 1930 and 1935? You were still at the studio, right?

BC: Yeah.

DJ: How come there was so little work? Because all of the cartoons were [with] sound, so they would have needed you.

BC: They had two other sound men.

DJ: Who were they?

BC: One came from New York. He was the original number-one sound man: his name was Bill Garity. He was a very good engineer. Funny thing was, we built most of the Disney sound equipment in the early days and he couldn't build anything, but he could sure design it. He was awkward as could be when he tried to build anything. The things that he did build worked after a fashion, but another fellow and I rebuilt pretty near everything he did.

DJ: Who was that?

BC: His name was Charles Slyfield. He was sound director at the studio for many years.

DJ: When you say you built things, what did you build?

BC: All the sound recording equipment.

DJ: You mean, even the microphones, too.

BC: No, it didn't include the microphones. That's a very special aspect.

DJ: But what did it include?

BC: It included all the amplifiers. Bill Garity designed a sound camera for recording sound on photographic film. A machine shop built it and had Caltech dynamically balance it to give good smooth motion. It worked pretty well. In a way it was illegal, because RCA and Western Electric had all the patents on that kind of equipment. Because we were a small outfit they more or less tolerated us, but actually, as I understood, we were violating a number of their patents. They used to come over and visit the studio, especially on Hyperion and Melrose, and kind of gently persuade Roy that, "We could sue you, but we'll give you a little more time. You better buy our equipment or rent it or lease [it]." And Roy would say, "We just can't afford it." So they tolerated it for quite awhile, until the money came in from *Snow White*. [Then] they signed up a contract with RCA and got their equipment and that was the end of our home-made equipment. But they went along for quite awhile on making the cartoons and making all these serials and everything on that equipment we built.

DJ: So when *Snow White* started in production, what job were you doing regarding the movie? You said you were doing film editing?

BC: Film editing, yeah.

DJ: What about the sound effects for *Snow White*? Were you involved in that, too?

BC: I was involved in that, but only after it was on the film.

JD: Jim MacDonald did a lot of the sound effects.

BC: Practically all of them, yeah.

DJ: So you didn't work with him, then?

BC: Not at that time, no. Later on, of course, I was there all the time. But at that time I just did film editing. All this material that was on the film I handled, but I didn't work in the production of it. Of course, first there was all the testing to be done. Trying to find the right voice for Snow White.

DJ: Were you there when they were doing that?

BC: Oh, yeah.

DJ: Can you talk a little bit about that?

BC: [For] *Snow White* particularly, Walt's animators and directors and everybody ... nobody exactly had but [a vague idea] about the particular voice quality that Walt wanted. So we had an endless number of people come in to try out, mostly young singers. Some we judged to be very good, but [they] didn't suit the part because their voice was too old or it was too well trained. Walt didn't want a professional voice, but yet he wanted a singer that could sing on pitch, and in his mind he knew exactly what he wanted in a voice quality, and everybody else was trying to find it for him and not having much luck until [Adriana] Caselotti came. [It was] undoubtedly the most difficult female voice we ever recorded.

DJ: Were you there when she first came there?

BC: Oh, yes.

DJ: What was your impression when she first walked in?

BC: She was a very attractive gal, but the first time I heard her sing I said, "Oh, my God!" Her voice was what Walt called girlish, but untrained. She came from a very musical family. I forget exactly what her father was.

DJ: He was an opera singer and teacher.

BC: Walt heard her and he said it, "This is it!" Everybody looked at each other and ... [raises eyebrows]. And the sound man said, "Oh, my God!" As it ended up, she was there days and days and days recording and [for a] day's work, maybe we'd get a few pieces we could use. That was where I got into editing, putting these pieces together, trying to make one continuous sound that was believable.

DJ: Now were you also there when she was recording these pieces?

BC: Oh, yeah.

DJ: You were there in the recording sessions?

BC: Oh, yeah.

DJ: And the director would have been there, like Ham Luske?

BC: Oh, yes.

DJ: Telling her how he wanted the lines to be spoken, I believe.

BC: Try another one.

DJ: Do you remember anything specific about those [sessions]?

BC: They repeated it so often and then we'd run the dailies for Walt. Of course the film had to go to the laboratory to be developed and then the next day he'd hear them. Maybe he'd find some part he liked, but discard the rest [and say] try again. One of those things. She'd come in again and we would try the parts he didn't like and sometimes he'd come down there himself, make a few comments. Bit by bit, little pieces by little pieces.... Occasionally we even took a word out of one take and put it in another one. This is all mechanical: first finding the word and finding whether you could [cut] it out or not without making a bump. And then we had to cooperate with the sound men so this would all smooth out somehow to sound like one performance.

DJ: You mentioned that she was undoubtedly the most difficult voice that they had recorded. Can you talk a little bit about that? Why it was so difficult?

BC: She had a voice range ... it was almost like a shriek, a lot of it, for one thing. And her sound level was almost completely uncontrolled. Then she'd blast one word or two and then go down to a very weak voice rendition. With an orchestral background we knew it just wouldn't work, so we would try to get the high points down and the low points up, and we tried to do that some and try to do that in the performance, too. But, of course, if you inflict too much of that on the singer, that hurts the performance. Because then they're not trying to sing the song beautifully, but they're trying to do a mechanical thing. So it was a great compromise in there. That's what made her difficult. Her voice was in a register that didn't record well in the first place. Some people just stand there and record beautifully with hardly any adjustment of the sound equipment, and others it's quite a battle sometimes.

Best voice I ever recorded in my life was Nelson Eddy. I could set the sound equipment and walk away. He just recorded beautifully.

DJ: I know that Walt had a speaker in his office so that he could listen to the Snow White auditions without seeing the person. Were you involved in setting that equipment up?

BC: I don't remember they had that for *Snow White*, though.

DJ: I remember reading about that many times. They had a speaker system in his office that was hooked up to the mike.

BC: I helped put it in.

DJ: Oh, you did?

BC: Oh, yeah.

DJ: Because he didn't want to be influenced by the way the girl looked, he just wanted to hear the voice.

BC: That's the story, anyway. I don't think that's accurate. Somebody picked that up and used it.

DJ: What really happened, then?

BC: I remember a very embarrassing situation. The directors and the top animators often times would confer with Walt, and after Walt left would say, "I wonder what he meant by that?" They were afraid to ask him, really. And one day we had a number of directors down there and Walt came down and made quite a few comments and then disappeared, went back to his office. He got to his [office and] he turned this thing on and Dave Hand said, "Boy, any of you got any idea of what he meant by that?" And several of them said, "I think he meant this." And Ham Luske said, "Nah, I think he meant this." [Walt] couldn't resist it. It was also a talk circuit, and nobody knew that he could talk to the stage. He said, "No, that was not what I meant at all!" And that gave it away. When we installed that he said, "I don't want anybody to know about this." But he couldn't resist when they started saying, "What did he mean?" He got on there and said, "No, that wasn't what I meant at all!" And everybody got red, because they wondered what they had said in previous recording [sessions] and whether he was monitoring [them]. [Laughs]

DJ: Were there any temper tantrums on the set of *Snow White* that you remember, or emotional scenes where somebody couldn't do it right and they broke down and cried or anything that dramatic that you can recall?

BC: No, I can't say that I do, no. Some of our patience was down pretty thin, but I don't remember any really dramatic things like that.

DJ: Do you remember Lucille LaVerne, who did the voice of the queen and the witch?

BC: Oh, yeah. Because that was no problem, that worked very well.

DJ: Were you there that day when she [read] both parts?

BC: Yeah, I probably was.

DJ: Do you remember Lucille LaVerne holding her glasses by the lenses and they would be always covered with fingerprints? Do you remember that?

BC: Yeah.

DJ: Very eccentric woman.

BC: She was, but very talented.

DJ: Could you talk a little bit more about her?

BC: I knew when they found her they thought, "No doubt about it, this is the one we want." They tried a number of different voices for the queen, I remember.

DJ: You [agreed] that she was eccentric. Was there any other evidence of that, other than holding her glasses?

BC: No, it was kind of subtle. There was something about her bearing, I don't know, that just seemed like she was ... and comments she made and so on. She seemed a little eccentric.

DJ: She must have had a good sense of humor.

BC: Oh, yeah. Some of the artists that they had sometimes would start laughing at their own performance when they'd hear it played back. It would strike them as funny. They surprised themselves. They'd say, "Well, gee, I really don't think I can do this," and when they heard it played back they'd crack up in laughter. Walt was a great one to take people that tended to say, "I can't do it," and he'd say, "Oh, yeah, sure you can. Do it!" And when somebody said, "This can't be done," he'd say, "When can we start on it?" That was his attitude with the parks and everything.

DJ: Getting back to *Snow White*. Do you recall if they tried to find a voice for Dopey and couldn't and that's why Dopey didn't have one or, from the beginning, was Dopey always going to have no voice?

BC: I'm not really sure about this, but as I recall at first they were trying to find a voice for Dopey and it just seemed like nothing would fit that character. Finally, somebody said, "Maybe we could make him funny without a voice." I think it was Wilfred Jackson, the cartoon director. I remember that [Jackson] acted out the parts of Dopey.

DJ: What about some of the other voices for the dwarfs.

BC: Of course, Pinto Colvig did two of them.

DJ: Grumpy and Sleepy. Doc was Roy Atwell. And Happy was Otis Harlin. Sneezy was done by Billy Gilbert.

BC: He was a well-known radio personality.

DJ: And Harry Stockwell was the one who sang the prince.

BC: His voice was good for the part, but later on we ran out of money. And that's the one thing that almost killed Walt as that animation of the prince was done last and because of lack of funds when the banks wouldn't give Walt any more money, [they] finally had to put the picture out with the prince that Walt didn't like and the animation was so bad. Walt never quite got over that. The rest of the picture was so good and that was the last thing: the animation on the prince was not good.

DJ: When was the last time you saw *Snow White*, do you remember?

BC: I saw it on TV once. It'd be quite a long time ago. I later became head of the sound department and I knew a lot about film and film preservation from working in the editorial department. We made so many prints of *Snow White*, of course, after it started. I knew the film must be getting scratched and deteriorating. So I talked to the manager of the studio and I said, "I really feel the need to preserve the sound track on *Snow White*, because that film, I know, is not in good shape anymore." Nitrate film also shrinks and eventually gets to a point where it won't even run on a standard machine, the sprocket holes won't match due to shrinkage. He said, "Yeah, if you want to, go ahead." It was really worse than I thought it was when I got the film out.

DJ: When was this?

BC: It was probably about 1967 or somewhere around there. So I did it one reel at a time.

DJ: Did you use the original negative or a positive print?

BC: I couldn't use the negative. The first thing I did was get Technicolor's protective master, and that had shrunk and was not in good shape, either. It had quite a bit of noise in it. It's a [garbled] film which was inherently noisy. And then I got looking for prints and I found some prints that were just plain dirty and by cleaning them up finally I got to a point where they were acceptable. Then with more modern sound equipment I could correct some of the flaws in the voices and in the recording in general, too. I finally got a better sound track than the original, in my opinion at least.

DJ: Can you tell me how that was done?

BC: I went to every source that could think of, including Technicolor— everything we had in stock in our vaults and all of that. It really had me stumped, and finally I got the idea I could check with the film exchanges in the big cities in the country to see if they could find a good print that was hardly used at all. And the exchange supervisor finally called me and said, "I found a print of that reel in Chicago that had only been run once."

DJ: What reel was it?

BC: It was in the middle of the picture, I don't know exactly.

DJ: How many reels were there? Six?

BC: I think it was six. So they rushed that to me and as luck would have it, it must have been well preserved in a cool place.

DJ: Was this from the original 1937 release, this print?

BC: 1937. Yes.

DJ: And this print was only shown once?

BC: Yeah. That particular reel. Sometimes the projectionist would tear up a reel and order another replacement they'd exchange with. This probably was one of those reels that was supposed to be a replacement and then they didn't use it or something like that.

DJ: Oh, how lucky.

BC: I really felt like I hit the jackpot, and that was the final thing that I needed to make a real good soundtrack with the material I had.

DJ: What is the process you use to re-record it but not lose the quality of the original, because often when you re-record something, the next generation is not as clear.

BC: That's [thanks] to improved equipment, sound equipment that we call equalizers.

DJ: Did you record it with a microphone? How did you re-record it?

BC: Directly from the film. We run the film soundtrack reproducer and electrically take it off … the sound signal is on the film, the lines … they take that off, and instead of reproducing it on a loud speaker, we put it into the recording mixing equipment and there it's amplified again and treated with an equalizer to improve things some. We also had a good cleaning process, which we didn't have originally, and besides that I personally hand-painted out some of the pops that were in there. These were specks of dirt. On the black soundtrack [they] would fend through white and when they passed the photocell it'd make a pretty sharp pop, which was distracting. I found a process, some years back, in 1940, where there was an ink that we could mix ourselves. I wrote the formula for it. And then with a very fine paintbrush and sometimes a spray gun, too, we could paint these pops out without affecting the sound.

DJ: You do it right on the film itself.

BC: Right on the film itself. Very meticulous job. I personally did some of that, too, where there were a few pops that nobody could originally take the time to get out.

DJ: You mentioned about the prince being badly drawn. After the movie came out, part of the prince was re-photographed and inserted into the negative. One scene was at the beginning: he's riding on his horse and there was always a loud pop.... I remember watching this movie as a child, and then in 1967, 1968, when it came out again I was waiting for the pop and there was no pop.

BC: I painted that.

DJ: That's one that you evidently had gotten out.

BC: Yeah.

DJ: Since then there's never been a pop, and there was also a pop somewhere else I recall—something to do with one of the scenes with the queen, I think. I remember that they had cleared that one up, too. It's interesting that you are the one that was responsible.

BC: I personally painted those out.

DJ: Very interesting.

BC: I did the same thing on *Fantasia*. I spent many weekends painting pops out of *Fantasia*.

DJ: Were there any special effects where they had trouble getting what they wanted?

BC: Walt was very fussy about that. The echo coming out of the well ... I remember we had difficulty with that for a while, and finally we found that by setting up a loud speaker and a microphone in the girls' toilet we could get that effect. So, after hours, when there were no girls around, at nighttime we set that up and got that echo effect.

DJ: Why the girls' toilet and not the boys' toilet?

BC: We tried everything, every toilet and everything we could in the place, and that one happened to work the best. Acoustically, that's a very difficult thing to get the way you want it. We tried all the others and somebody said, "No girls around now, let's try the girls' toilet." And that worked beautifully.

DJ: You just used the film of Caselotti singing and then you re-recorded it.

BC: We'd take that original "I'm Wishing" and shoot it through a loudspeaker in the girls' toilet and pick it up with a microphone. It was very reverberant in there.

DJ: Did any of them ever know it?

BC: Oh, yes.

DJ: Were you there when they were filming some of the live action?

BC: Oh, yeah, dancing and so on.

DJ: Do you remember the woman who did the live action for Snow White, Marge Belcher?

BC: Oh, yeah, that was Art Babbitt's wife.

DJ: Marge Belcher at the time.

BC: Yeah, she was quite a good dancer.

DJ: So you were there during some of that filming as well. I was told that for the queen there was a young woman there and I just found out recently that she later stayed at the studio and she married Jack Boyd. She worked in Special Effects. Her name was Jane Fowler. She modeled the queen.

BC: I remember a funny incident, too. I remember the incident where the person acting out the witch was dressed in a costume and everything and did the thing so well. Hal Adelquist was down there and he was kind of Walt's leg-man. When she got to this part, "My heart, my heart, my heart…. Give me a glass of water," Hal thought she was having a heart attack. So did I, actually.

DJ: That was Lucille LaVerne when she was actually reading the part from the script.

BC: That's it. Yeah. So I ran for a glass of water and everybody thought she was having a heart attack.

DJ: Now the one who's acting it out would follow the soundtrack of the one who did the vocal, they told me, and there would be a click track and they would count, and the voice would start and they would mouth the words and then act out the parts. Do you recall that?

BC: Oh, yeah, I prepared those click tracks. It was part of my editing job, too.

DJ: I know for some of the dwarfs that some of the animators would come in and [act for the live-action reference].

BC: Oh, yeah. And Walt was pretty good at that, too, using people on the lot. In his mind, he could visualize some of these people that were on the lot that weren't performers at all. He'd say, "I bet you could do that."

DJ: When you were doing *Snow White*, did anybody ever ask you to act any of the things out?

BC: No.

DJ: You were just always a participant?

BC: Always, in the background somewhere, yeah. I remember my first editing job. It was the entertainment sequence, three-hundred-and-thirty-seven feet long, where they danced around and Dopey was on Sneezy's [shoulders]. That sequence was my first complete thing on *Snow White* that I edited and put all the parts together.

DJ: What was the sound effect when Sneezy blew off Dopey?

BC: It was a compressed air thing, as I remember, that Jimmy MacDonald cooked up.

DJ: He was really brilliant, wasn't he?

BC: Oh, what a talent. Besides being an excellent musician, he was a very good drummer. He could take those musical scores and interpret things and time them out and he was pretty close to a genius himself.

DJ: I asked him about some of the sound effects. Did he do the drumming of Dopey or did he have somebody else do that?

BC: Most likely he did it, I'm thinking. [This was almost certainly done by Eddie Forrest, one of the Disney soundmen.]

DJ: He mentioned a couple of other names for people that were in that little band. And for the organ they used a real organ and then a glass filled with water, to blow on it, to give it more of an antique kind of sound.

BC: I think that was the organ we had on the stage in Hyperion. Yeah, they bought an organ and I think we used that one. Later on, for *20,000 Leagues*, we went downtown to a big theater downtown and got a good organist and recorded down there.

DJ: You were probably involved when they recorded the score on the soundstage with the orchestra.

BC: Yes.

DJ: Did Frank Churchill do his own orchestrations? And Paul Smith? Or do you think they had other people score them?

BC: Paul Smith did some of his own, I know. I don't recall that Frank Churchill did.

DJ: I know he wasn't sober very often.

BC: He liked his liquor, but, for instance, on *Three Little Pigs*, he got a fifth of whiskey and sat down and wrote the whole score for *Three Little Pigs* in one afternoon. Got good and relaxed, shut the doors, and went in there and.... Very talented guy. I worked with him in radio, too.

DJ: Yeah, he was the staff pianist at KMTR.

BC: He had a great knack for timing, besides. Everything he did usually was melodic and basically simple. You could go out of the theater whistling his tunes. He had a miraculous sense of timing. I don't know how familiar you are with beats that we had: a ten beat or twelve beat, and so on. He'd look out of the window at some fellow walking down the street and he'd say, "He's walking in twelves," which meant a twelve beat. He'd turn around and put on the metronome and set it on twelve and the guy would be right in step. Uncanny sense of timing.

I remember one morning, in the sweatbox [session], there was a section which was way out of sync. Whoever edited that made a big mistake. Not just a little bit but a good sized one, and Churchill looked out and he'd call the projectionist and say, "Pull that soundtrack down toward the bottom magazine twenty-eight frames." So he counted out to twenty-eight frames, pulled it down, backed it up, and he ran it again and it was exactly in sync.

DJ: I'll be damned.

BC: I never found anybody that could do that in all the experience I ever had with musicians.

DJ: That wouldn't have been in *Snow White*?

BC: No, it wasn't.

DJ: Amazing.

BC: Uncanny. And then to demonstrate it again he'd look at something else that was going that had some kind of a beat to it or some film where a horse was walking and he'd say, "He's walking in eights." He got a kick out of demonstrating it.

DJ: Larry Morey wrote the lyrics for the songs in *Snow White*. But he also worked on some of the story parts. Do you recall which?

BC: I don't know which parts, no. He did a lot of writing for *Bambi* that pleased Walt very much. In fact, Walt doubled his salary in one week. And Larry said, "Walt, this is going overboard." Walt said, "No, no, no, no. I'm very pleased in your working." And he doubled his salary in one week.

DJ: How much salary were you getting during *Snow White*?

BC: Seventy-five dollars a week.

DJ: You were? That was a lot of money then, in 1937. You could live quite well.

BC: I was doing pretty well. But then, not for the hours I put in.

DJ: Because you were working all the time.

BC: Unlimited hours. A lot of time, Sundays, Saturdays, night, days, any time.

DJ: Were you at the premiere of Snow White?

BC: Oh, yeah.

DJ: What was impression when you saw the movie for the first time?

BC: Oh yeah, sure. It [was at] Carthay Circle.

DJ: Can you tell me about it?

BC: Well, I was just thrilled to death. I could feel the audience, the mass reaction to it. And they had this beautiful set-up out in front with the *Snow White* characters on this long walkway before you get to the theater. It was before Christmas and everybody was in the right mood, too. By the time they got up to the box office a lot of them were enchanted already. It was really quite a set-up. It didn't take long before you could feel that mass reaction. I was just thrilled to death, even though I had only a very small part in putting it together. The way the audience ate it up was really something. The hand they got at the end, that was really the icing on the cake.

DJ: Was it spontaneous?

BC: You bet, and it didn't stop for quite awhile, either. The next day, Walt came in the sweatbox [and] he looked tired. I suppose he'd been celebrating some, too. But he didn't look particularly happy and Dave Hand said, "Walt, you be should happier than you are," or something like that. Walt said, "How in the hell are we ever going to top this?" Not equal it, but top it. [That was] kind of his philosophy: everything he did he wanted the next one to be better. I always remember that we thought, "Boy he'd come in floating on air." And he looked a little concerned, saying, "How in the hell are we ever going to top this?"

DJ: That was the very next day?

BC: The next day.

DJ: In some ways they never did top it.

BC: True. It was completely different material, but it still had some kind of a magic touch to it that the others didn't.

DJ: Did you go to the party, the famous party that they had shortly after *Snow White*?

BC: No, I wasn't invited to that.

DJ: It was a weekend. You didn't go to that?

BC: No, I wasn't invited to that.

DJ: It was maybe a couple of months later. Some people said it was extremely wild, other people said it was beautiful.

BC: I went to a few Christmas parties that were wild. One where they wrecked the grand piano.

DJ: Oh, is that right? You mean on the soundstage?

BC: No, this was downtown on Seventh Street, some restaurant down there. Frank Churchill, I remember, was really oiled up.

DJ: What happened?

BC: They started throwing things around and they had a couple of gals dancing on top of the piano and it was really a wild one. They had another Christmas party.... The last one they had was down on Riverside Drive at the Breakfast Club and then Walt called it off.

DJ: Was this before the war or after the war?

BC: I think it was before the war.

DJ: Now, he'd go to these parties, too, Walt did?

BC: Usually not.

DJ: Oh, no?

BC: No.

DJ: Because I understand he liked to drink, too?

BC: Oh yeah. But he didn't like to mix with the common herd too much in these parties. He always—I don't know—was afraid. I remember the Ben Sharpsteen retirement party. Ben had really been a contributor, a whole lot of the success of the cartoons. Very good director and brought some of these animators up to where they were really good. And Walt felt very indebted to him, I'm sure. So they threw a nice, big party for Ben Sharpsteen and they invited Walt. And I'll have to go back a little bit. Walt was criticizing the directors and one time he said, "I'm going to take one of these stories and direct it myself and show you what I mean." And that was *The Golden Touch*. Anyway, Walt got there a little later than I did and the party was going pretty good and quite a few drinks had been consumed. Walt said hello to the guys and shook hands with Ben and got pictures taken and everything. And one man in there said, "Hey, Walt, remember *The Golden Touch*?" And Walt said, "Don't you ever mention that again." He was mad, I mean, really cross. Then another one picked it up and with that Walt turned around and walked out, went home.

Interviewed on January 26, 1990.

Eloise Tobelman (1908–1996)

Eloise Tobleman was hired on August 14, 1935, as a steno-typist. She spent the next 30 years of her career working for Disney. By the time she retired, on February 4, 1966, she was working as a film librarian.

Eloise Tobleman: I'm eighty two.

David Johnson: You're in the prime of life. ... I would like to know a little about your background. I know you went to Mills College. Where you were born, and how you came to the Disney Studio.

ET: I was born in Arizona before it was a state. That's where those Indian baskets came from [pointing to them]. They're pretty valuable. They're almost eighty years old. And an artist that went to the studio did that painting. I wanted to be a newspaper woman. I took English at college and my dad was a mining engineer. He was in Africa, in Rhodesia. And he let me have a student tour of Europe when I graduated. When I got through, everybody went home and I was in Paris by myself. This was in the thirties. I graduated in 1930. The folks said I could come down to Africa. That's what I really wanted to do. Meantime I talked to a woman of the Café de Paris, and she'd been to Mills and she heard about this. She was studying French at the Sorbonne. So I invited her to come along. She was wealthy. Her family owned big hotels. We had a great time. We called ourselves the "Cape to Cairo Chess Club" because we learned to play chess on the way.

DJ: There were just two of you?

ET: Yeah.

DJ: How long was this adventure?

ET: She just stayed a month or so, but I was there about three months and my folks were there a year. Then Dad had to go back on the west coast [of Africa], because that was quicker—seventeen days. But Mother and I went out to the other coast, the east coast.

DJ: Zanzibar?

ET: Yeah. [We] got on a German ship and it took thirty-seven days, because it carried people and cargo and stopped at a lot of ports. Great, great trip. And ended up in Hamburg.

DJ: So you ended up in Hamburg?

ET: Yeah. And we ended up this whole business in Salt Lake City, where Dad had been working before he got this offer from Africa. I went down to the newspaper and told them I'd just come back from Africa which had fabulous copper mines. Of course, Salt Lake has them, too. I tried to sell myself to be taken on as a reporter, but the editor said, "We just have one woman and that's enough. She does the society column." I did sell them on the idea of writing a story of Rhodesia, a column. I spent three days on it because I had to get everything from Dad. It wasn't how he lived or how he liked it: it was about the copper mines, graded copper and how it was going to be mined, and all of this. I gave him a picture, a snapshot which they blew up like that. It was a truck going through one of those termite hills that'd been cut to make room for the road. That's how big they were, and that's how many there were, because they couldn't go around all of them. They printed the picture and the editor said I could get my check downstairs. I went down and it was for $3 [laughs] and even in those days that wasn't very much. So I just walked up the street to the Mormon Business College and enrolled in the steno-typing. I worked at that and then a classmate of mine talked me into coming out here to visit her and maybe get a job. She said it was great to work at the studios. They paid more.

DJ: How long did it take you to learn stenography?

ET: I guess it took a year. You know what a steno-type is?

DJ: No, I have no idea.

ET: Court reporters. Except the court reporters have a great big tray so they can put a bigger pad of notes.

DJ: How does it work?

ET: It's a code. These are the vowels so you can write part of a word or a whole word of two or three words.

DJ: But are they written in English. I mean is it written so that I could understand it?

ET: No. But you could learn to read it without having to learn to write it, of course. We had a court … a stenographer at Disney's that became a court reporter. And she took that Robert Kennedy/Sirhan Sirhan trial. But like lots of court reporters, the pressure was so strong she started having martinis at noon.

DJ: So then you came out to Los Angeles.

ET: Yeah.

DJ: How long did it take before you got a job?

ET: This didn't take too long, because I had heard that Disney wanted steno-typists. But they said, "That was six or eight months ago, it would've been taken care of." I was telling this to the brother of the classmate who had invited me out here, and he said, "Why don't we call up Walt?" [Laughs] So he looked it up and dialed and he said, "Walt, please." Awfully, real nervy guy. Of course he got Walt's secretary who, it turned out, hired people at that time, I mean good ones.

DJ: What year was this?

ET: It was August 1935.

DJ: Now was this Carolyn Shafer who was his secretary?

ET: No, Dolores Voght. I told her that I wasn't too good on a machine, but I'd get better. I guess I said the right thing because she said she'd try me for two weeks.

DJ: Without pay?

ET: No. They paid $25 a week, which is huge. She never did tell me whether I was permanent or not. I stayed 31 years. [Laughs]

DJ: When you went the first day, did you meet Walt that same day?

ET: Oh, goodness no!

DJ: When did you finally meet him?

ET: We weren't assigned to directors. We sat in a pool. There was a woman from Canada, a large woman who was in charge of the files. [There was] a great bank of files and a wooden fence and then the five of us with desks and typewriters. They called them when they wanted somebody. And she had a nervous tick and her head kept bobbing, and she looked down the line on us to see who to send.

DJ: What would you do when you were waiting?

ET: We always had stuff to type. I don't know, maybe it was for the front office, maybe we just sat and fooled around. [Laughs]

DJ: You said there was only one other steno-typist?

ET: Yes, but there were three [stenographers].

DJ: So there were five of you altogether.

ET: Yeah. It started out with just one woman and Walt was getting ready to do something ... you could tell that because he was hiring shorthand writers and he had these action analysis classes....

DJ: Yes, Don Graham.

ET: I took those.

DJ: I have some of those.

ET: In the back of that book by Frank Thomas and Ollie Johnston there's one that I took. It's got "ET." Ham Luske gave it. It was all about the movement of drapery. ... You say stenographer and actually we never took dictation.

DJ: Right. You took the story meetings.

ET: We took projection room notes.

DJ: The sweatbox. Go back to when you were first there. When did you finally meet Walt?

ET: I was sent up there to take notes and he was talking to a layout man, just the two of them. I suppose he said hello or sit down or something. But he didn't dictate. I think he said I should take notes on their discussion. And they were examining this layout. They talked about the changes they'd make. And then when they were through Walt said to me, "Tell me what we're gonna do." I could have told him without the notes, but I took down the notes and told him. He seemed satisfied, so I guess that was my test.

DJ: Did you take this machine? Were you doing it on this machine?

ET: Yep. That's the only kind of shorthand I can do.

DJ: Going back to *Snow White*: are there any moments you can recall during the making of that picture that stick out in your memory?

ET: I think when Walt threw out a whole sequence, that really made everybody stand up! The soup sequence. … He thought about *every-thing* day and night and all the time!

DJ: He did?

ET: I remember one time I'd lost or misplaced my wallet and I didn't find it out till I got out to the car and then I came back in to see if I'd left it in the unit someplace. I walked across the hall and it was all empty except Walt was sitting there staring at the storyboards. And I think he did a lot of that.

DJ: Did he ever call you up in the middle of the night or anything and say, "We need a steno-typist, we're having a meeting"?

ET: [Laughs] No. But if we were still in the steno pool, he would write notes on paper napkins at lunch. Or he'd use a dictaphone and send down the cylinders for us to transcribe. The first person in was supposed to get these things and start typing. We tried not to be first, because they were awfully hard to do. Because he wasn't clear when he spoke. He didn't speak clearly and he wasn't too good with words. He acted things out better than he spoke.

DJ: In other words, he wasn't an articulate man.

ET: Yeah. The story conferences were full of that where he acted things out and that was kind of hard to put down and still get on with the next thing. [Laughs]

DJ: You played golf with Ham Luske?

ET: Yes, and his wife and his assistant.

DJ: Who was his assistant?

ET: Rusty Jones.

DJ: Was Ham a good golfer?

ET: Yes, he was, but he liked to play practical jokes, especially on me.

DJ: What kind of jokes?

ET: He'd exchange my golf ball for one that went into a thousand pieces when I hit it. [Laughs] I managed to find a ball that wouldn't roll straight and kind of went off like that. I brought it with me to the course and then I didn't have the nerve to put it down. I gave it to Rusty and he was happy to do it. So we got to a hole [and] Ham hit a real long ball, but often out into the rough and this went way out in the trees.

DJ: Where was this golf course?

ET: Griffith Park. Six o'clock in the morning. Saturday! So we got to the green and Ham was back in the trees. And here came this ball out of the trees way up in the air and it landed right on the green. Rusty hurried over there and put my ball that wouldn't roll straight in place of Ham's. Ham came up there and at first I thought he knew. But I guess not. He was too intent on making four. He wanted to get close enough with this long putt to sink the next one and get a par. So he looked at it from a lot of different angles and then he hit it and this crazy thing.... [Laughs] And we just could hardly stand it. We managed not to laugh out loud and he said, "I must have tried to steer it!" [Laughs] Ham was a great guy to blame everything on himself. If things didn't go right, it was his fault.

[About Ward Kimball:] He was loud, and he was profane, and he was messy. One time he came in the sweatbox, they called him up, and he came in eating something. When I left, all down this nice clean shiny hall were these wrappers from this candy bar and what-not. That's the kind of guy he was. Messy.

[About Hugh Henessy:] He was very quiet and very industrious and had a nice sense of humor. When I think of Hugh Henessy I think of him coming into the room I was in when he was in my unit. He had a pencil about an inch long and he said, "Could I get some more of these?"[Laughs] He had it in a holder, I guess. That's the way he was. That was [his] humor and his nature, too, to be conservative and a very nice fellow.

DJ: He was a newspaper illustrator before he came to the studio.

ET: Was he?

DJ: Yeah, he and Charlie Philippi were both newspaper men.

ET: At the old studio, I remember when we didn't have over-time pay but we just took time off when we could. I was going down the stairs one afternoon, kinda early, and Walt came along, amd he's going down the stairs, too. He said, "Where are you going?" I said, "I'm going over to Griffith Park to play the nine-hole course." He said "You should really go in the morning. It's much nicer," and he started to sell me on the fact that early morning was better than early evening. That's the way he was. That's pretty nice.

DJ: You never saw him in a story session arguing with somebody else?

ET: No, because nobody would argue with *him*.

DJ: Do you remember Fred Moore?

ET: I know him as one of the animators. He was in sweatboxes. He was a great one to take good care of his clothes, and he put his feet up on the chair in front and looked at his socks to see how they looked. [Laughs] It seemed like that. Maybe he wouldn't draw all day; he'd be fooling around. But maybe late in the afternoon he suddenly got the inspiration or the desire or something and he'd draw furiously.

DJ: He was another one that hit the bottle too much.

ET: Like Frank Churchill. You know, I was standing at one end of the hall one time and he was pressing the button for the [elevator]. I just happened to look down there and here was this elegant [man]. He was beautifully attired all the time, with the complete suit and hat. He was trying to push this button and he was drunk. That's the way I think of Frank. But on the other hand, if he was in a story conference, Walt called him in and said what kind of thing they were going to do, and ask him if he had any ideas and he could turn to the piano and just play a few notes.

DJ: Even when he was bombed?

ET: He wouldn't be bombed then. But he was so quick to get the idea of what was wanted and so good, turning out all those pieces of music. He was an artist.

Interviewed on February 10, 1990.

Thor Putnam
(1911–2001)

Thor Putnam attended Stanford University with Frank Thomas, Ollie Johnston, and James Algar, and all four men shared apartments while studying at the Chouinard Art Institute in Los Angeles. Each found employment at Disney in 1934–35. Putnam became a top art director/layout artist on *Pinocchio*, *Fantasia*'s "Bald Mountain" and "Ave Maria" segments, and many other features and television shows as well as *The Little House* and *Ben and Me*.

Thorington Caldwell Putnam was born October 14, 1911, in Berkeley, California. He graduated from Stanford University in 1932, studied illustration with Pruett Carter from 1932 to 1934, and joined the Disney Studio in 1934 in Layout. He served as assistant layout man on *Snow White* and *Ferdinand the Bull*, then became head of Layout on *Pinocchio*. He worked on all subsequent productions in that capacity until 1942, when he joined the U.S. Navy for active duty (June 1, 1942 to October 2, 1946).

While in the Navy he supervised the production of thirty-seven U.S. Navy training films and photographic reports, covering a wide variety of both technical and of dramatic naval topics. Thor was often responsible for all phases of production, including the script.

On November 4, 1946, Thor rejoined the Disney Studio in the layout department and worked on all animated features from *Melody Time* to *Lady and the Tramp* and on many shorts.

Thor Putnam left Disney on March 13, 1959, and died January 26, 2001.

David Johnson: You were there when *Snow White* was actually in the planning stage.

Thor Putman: Yes.

DJ: Do you recall your reaction when you first found out that they were doing this feature film?

TP: I recall a sort of a key meeting when Walt himself called us in. See, the studio was over on Hyperion Avenue at that time and I recall that there weren't probably more than about three or four hundred people working at Disney's then. [By end of the summer of 1934 there were approximately 200–225 people in total.] He called them in to the soundstage and gave us sort of an extemporaneous speech about [how] we're going to make this feature. As I recall it was one of the times that I realized how really talented he was. He then started acting out some of the dwarfs in pantomime. I suddenly realized why this man cannot only do story but he can act as well.

DJ: Do you recall anything specific?

TP: I do. He was getting down to Bashful, one of the dwarfs. And he went into a sort of pantomime about how he would react if Snow White kissed him on top of his head. That was done so well that I always remember that little sequence. Like [he'd] cringe a little bit. He did that. But then everybody thought, "Oh, my God...." Here's this little studio and we knew right off the bat it was going to be very expensive. Everyone is [thinking], "Is this going to be a big flop?" I had the same feeling about Disneyland, when that came up. I thought, "Oh, my God, he's going to do it this time!" [Laughs] His enthusiasm came across. I mean he got everybody really interested in it.

I can recall that on that wishing well sequence and the castle, we did indeed do quite a bit of research on that castle. You couldn't do something like that out of your head.

DJ: What kind of research?

TP: I would say, as I recall, the [castle] in Segovia, [Spain,] sort of an alcazar there. This is very much like the one that's in the picture.

DJ: They used that in *Ferdinand, the Bull*, I remember, [for] the opening.

TP: I think it is, right. And I have a shot of it that I made later and I was surprised how much it did look like the one in Segovia.

One thing I was going to say about the Disney architecture generally, and this includes *Cinderella*: it's almost an architecture of its own. In effect, it's almost a non-architecture. Non-period. This isn't for example anything that's specific. Now the castle in *Cinderella* is nearer. I remember John Hench did an awful lot of the design of that and he just did it out of his head.

DJ: But you recall some research being done on *Snow White*'s castle.

TP: Oh, yes, I know I did. Oh, surely, the turrets....

DJ: Tell me more about that.

TP: Well, just whatever castle scraps we'd find. I don't think we did anything particularly on the wishing well.

DJ: But these turrets?

TP: That's right. I did research on that.

DJ: And the one you can think of is the Spain one.

TP: That's just for the distant shot.

DJ: Then what about these close-ups?

TP: I don't specifically remember by name just where that would be.

DJ: But you had photographs.

TP: Oh, yes.

DJ: Maybe some French chateaux.

TP: Yeah, that sort of thing. Yeah, there's no question about that. You always did that. And the studio did indeed have quite a good library with a lot of good reference in it. Just down the hall and you could always go there.

DJ: Now for this wishing well. Did you draw anything for the design of that?

TP: I remember really struggling. I don't know if it was an up-shot or a down-shot. I tried to get depth into this thing. In other words, bigger stones here and as you went down they get smaller and smaller and smaller.

DJ: That's when she's looking in the well.

TP: Yeah, looking in the well. I remember working real hard on that one. Because it's a hard thing to take a flat surface and to get a feeling of depth.

DJ: Now did you have photographs to assist you on that?

TP: Possibly stones. Just the appearance of stones might have been used on that. But other than that it's pretty much [Charles] Philippi leading the way he wanted it to look.

DJ: Including all of the vines.

TP: Oh, yes. That's right.

DJ: Even the bucket.

TP: Yeah, things like that. I was appalled [at] how he could pull this out of his head, [at] his ability to do that.

DJ: Do you recall using any sketches by Albert Hurter to help you?

TP: Yes, definitely.

DJ: Do you recall what some of those might have been?

TP: Let me see. I'll tell you another thing that happened. After having made a layout to go to camera or go to be painted, it was sort of a policy at that time to take a layout, a finalized sketch and send it to Hurter for him to look over. And he would. Very often he would take your sketch and not like something: [it] wasn't old enough, [it] didn't have the feeling that he was able to impart ... and he would work over your sketch.

DJ: Do you remember him working over yours?

TP: Yes, I do.

DJ: And what did he have to do about that?

TP: Very often he'd make it more aged than it was, than you had made it. And [add] more texture than possibly you had put into it. He had that ability, definitely. He had a certain touch and they wanted that. They wanted his ability to do that. It was important. I would say he was important.

DJ: Can you recall anything specific that on your design he changed that maybe at the time you didn't like but then realized that he was right?

TP: I would say specifically making stones look older, more character, maybe more rugged. He would actually just work right over your drawing with putting that kind of work on it.

DJ: And what about in the trees, in the flight through the forest.

TP: Yes, he worked on that.

DJ: Can you recall any changes he made on that?

TP: Branches sometimes, certain things that he just wanted to put his touch to. I'm glad you mentioned his name because I would definitely say that Albert Hurter contributed a lot to *Snow White*, and *Pinocchio*, too, later. For example, the way he realized the prince. As a matter of fact, he would be the first visualization of a sequence. He would come in and do stuff like that.

DJ: Now when you worked on the flight through the forest, do you recall going to any story meetings?

TP: We would attend, very often, story meetings, which Walt would come to. But I don't recall on that particular sequence, no. Very often the director and his layout man would attend story meetings.

DJ: Do you recall any *Snow White* story meetings you attended?

TP: Actually, I don't. It's funny, you'd think that I would, but I don't. I just remember that initial meeting that I told you [about, in which] Walt acted the whole story of *Snow White* out ... not literally, but his first announcement. Everybody remembers that meeting and that it was in the sound stage in the old studio. I think everybody was really impressed with the way he told it.

DJ: Ken Anderson told how Walt would even describe the marble of the queen's throne and how when the dwarfs were eating their soup how it tasted so much better because there was meat in it ... better than anything that they had ever made for themselves. Did Walt go into those details?

TP: He would talk like that. He would have that kind of an eye, mental picture. There's no question about that. Now a lot of the little touches that you see in all the Disney pictures, very often some of the things that are memorable are Walt's own ideas.

DJ: Is there anything from *Snow White* that you *know* was Walt's idea?

TP: I just remember that particular bit of pantomime where Bashful is being kissed on the top of his head by Snow White. I just remember his acting that out and it was so good. It was such a good bit of action.

DJ: What about Perce Pearce. I was told he really knew how to manipulate Walt.

TP: I remember him arriving at Disney's. He came from New York, I think, and I saw him go up the ladder. I saw him do just that, just one little step at a time, until he finally ended up being top storyman. And he was good. He had a good sense of humor. It's important for a storyman to talk, to get out there and really sell his story. And to do that he had almost to be an actor himself. I remember once, on *Pinocchio*, how T. Hee ran out of the door and around the hall and came in through the other door. Everybody died.

DJ: Would you say that Perce Pearce stole a lot of the ideas?

TP: No, I wouldn't. People might have thought that he did. Larry Morey was the lyricist for *Snow White* and they were very good friends. We just happened to have gone on a quick, one week or so vacation to Honolulu and they were both on the ship. So I got to know them quite well on that trip. This was after *Snow White*.

One of the things that you always noticed in all of the Disney pictures as you worked on them was how loose and how wonderful the pencil test looked and then how it all stiffened up, very often, as it got traced on cel. And a lot of the real good movement would just become stiff. It wouldn't retain the flow that the pencil tests had. I think everybody felt that.

I didn't feel so good about Snow White generally because I felt she was stiff and did look traced and didn't really become a factor as, say, the dwarfs did. She was pretty much a puppet moving around in many ways. I think most people feel that too. [The human characters in the earlier short] *Goddess of Spring* were just awful, poor, no question about it. And that was one of the things that you felt when he was attempting *Snow White*, and with *Goddess of Spring* in the background you wondered, "How is this going to come off?"

DJ: You went to Stanford?

TP: Yes.

DJ: Were you a fine arts major?

TP: I majored in English.

DJ: Did you start at the same time as Ollie and Frank?

TP: Pretty much the same time. I think Frank and I almost started the same week. And Ollie came in about a week or so later. [Note: In fact Frank began in September 1934 and Ollie came in in January 1935.] And Jim Algar was another one from Stanford. He did all the True-Life Adventures live-action nature pictures.

There's something to bear in mind and that's the appearance of the old studio. It was sort of like a rabbit hutch. It had different levels. It had different small rooms. The music rooms were sort of small. The individual animation rooms were little tiny cells. Nothing of the splendor of the Burbank place now. There was only one sound stage. Just one.

DJ: The walls were just cardboard?

TP: Oh, no, it wasn't as primitive as that, but they were little rooms all adjacent to each other. And you were so close, you were in such proximity (like when I was an assistant) that you knew everybody in the hall and everybody [else]. It was sort of like a family.

I'll tell you another thing. There's a lot of inner play and inner trading of ideas between the animators. They did a lot of this. They would touch [base] with each other, they would exchange ideas, they would ask advice. Ferguson was almost the senior man and everybody respected Norm Ferguson for his experience. So in other words, there was a lot of trading off between animators. More in the old studio than in the new. Because they were all, sort of, together. And the similarity of movement [that Snow White shows].... You didn't feel that when one music room stopped and another one picked up, you could never tell where it happened, because it flowed very well.

DJ: Did you know Walt very well?

TP: Everybody knew him quite well, but he was a distant person. He never, at least to most of the people, he didn't share too much. Even in a story meeting, he walked in and did it and walked out. I only went up to his home twice in the whole time. When I was in the Navy and in uniform, he invited all of us that were in active duty up to [his house], one time, on a Sunday. And once I was invited to his place in Holmby Hills where he finally lived.

Interviewed in Winter 1988.

Acknowledgments

Many individuals have given so generously of their time and energy to see this project through to fruition. Unfortunately, I know only three of them: my publisher Bob McLain, my editor Didier Ghez, and a Greek friend here in Athens, Christos Mitsios. The rest of you, I can only offer a blanket canopy of gratitude and appreciation for all your dedication and unflagging effort. Blessings to all!

About the Author

David Johnson is an authority on the Disney film *Snow White and the Seven Dwarfs*. A resident of Athens, Greece, he holds a masters (with distinction) in music from the Manhattan School of Music.

More Books from Theme Park Press

Theme Park Press is the largest independent publisher of Disney, Disney-related, and general interest theme park books in the world, with over 100 new releases each year.

We're always looking for new talent.

For a complete catalog, including book descriptions and excerpts, please visit:

ThemeParkPress.com

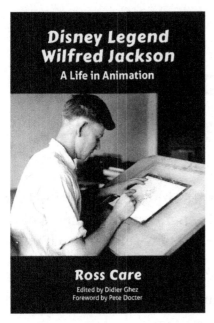

Directing Disney

Part diary, part correspondence, part historical essay, this unique book presents the life of Walt Disney's most acclaimed director, Wilfred Jackson, whose long career began with the earliest Mickey Mouse shorts and continued through Snow White, Lady and the Tramp, and many more.

themeparkpress.com/books/wilfred-jackson.htm

From Marceline to the Magic Kingdom

Award-winning Associate Press reporter Bob Thomas' original biography of Walt Disney is fast-moving and insightful-the perfect introduction to Walt for readers of all ages.

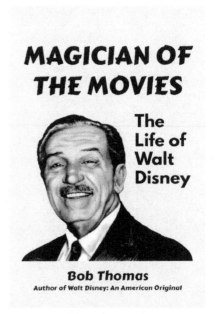

themeparkpress.com/books/magician-movies.htm

The Studio Life of a Disney Legend

Eric Larson, one of Walt Disney's famed "Nine Old Men", went to work at the studio in 1933 and left in 1986. He knew everyone at Disney who was anyone, and he kept a diary of the personalities, the pranks, and the politics. This is his warm, witty story.

themeparkpress.com/books/50-years-mouse-house.htm

Disney History from the Source

The Walt's People series is an oral history of all things Disney, as told by the artists, animators, designers, engineers, and executives who made it happen, from the 1920s through the present. Roy E. Disney, Jack Kinney, Alan Coats, and many more.

themeparkpress.com/books/walts-people-19.htm

An Encyclopedic Reference of Disney Comics

From the United States to Italy, from France and Spain to Brazil, Turkey, Russia, and beyond, noted comics historian Alberto Becattini traces the evolution of Disney comics around the world in the most authoritative, comprehensive treatment of the "Disney funnies" ever put into print.

themeparkpress.com/books/disney-comics.htm

Blame It on Gremlins?

In the 1940s, Walt Disney had his hands on a new film franchise involving gremlins, little creatures that caused mischief, mostly of the mechanical kind. But no gremlins film was ever made. Walt himself cancelled the project. This is the story of what went wrong. (And it wasn't gremlins.)

themeparkpress.com/books/gremlin-trouble.htm